Alan Titchmarsh
how to garden

Gardening in the Shade

Alan Titchmarsh
how to garden

Gardening in the Shade

BBC
BOOKS

10 9 8 7 6 5 4 3 2 1

Published in 2009 by BBC Books, an imprint of
Ebury Publishing, a Random House Group Company

The Random House Group Limited Reg. No. 954009

Addresses for companies within the Random House
Group can be found at
www.randomhouse.co.uk

The Random House Group Limited supports The Forest
Stewardship Council (FSC), the leading international
forest certification organisation. All our titles that are
printed on Greenpeace approved FSC certified paper
carry the FSC logo. Our paper procurement policy can
be found at www.rbooks.co.uk/environment

A CIP catalogue record for this book is available from
the British Library.

ISBN 978-1-84-6073953

Produced by Outhouse!
Shalbourne, Marlborough, Wiltshire SN8 3QJ

BBC BOOKS
COMMISSIONING EDITORS: Lorna Russell, Stuart Cooper
PROJECT EDITOR: Caroline McArthur
PRODUCTION CONTROLLER: Bridget Fish

OUTHOUSE!
CONCEPT DEVELOPMENT & PROJECT MANAGEMENT:
   Elizabeth Mallard-Shaw
CONTRIBUTING EDITOR: Jonathan Edwards
PROJECT EDITOR: Rebecca Snelling
ART DIRECTION: Sharon Cluett, Robin Whitecross
SERIES DESIGN: Sharon Cluett
DESIGNER: Heather McCarry

ILLUSTRATIONS by Lizzie Harper, except pages 32–5,
which are by Julia Brittain

PHOTOGRAPHS by Jonathan Buckley, except where
credited otherwise on page 128

Colour origination by Altaimage, London
Printed and bound by Firmengruppe APPL,
Wemdig, Germany

Contents

Introduction

Gardening is one of the best and most fulfilling activities on earth, but it can sometimes seem complicated and confusing. The answers to problems can usually be found in books, but big fat gardening books can be rather daunting. Where do you start? How can you find just the information you want without wading through lots of stuff that is not appropriate to your particular problem? Well, a good index is helpful, but sometimes a smaller book devoted to one particular subject fits the bill better – especially if it is reasonably priced and if you have a small garden where you might not be able to fit in everything suggested in a larger volume.

The *How to Garden* books aim to fill that gap – even if sometimes it may be only a small one. They are clearly set out and written, I hope, in a straightforward, easy-to-understand style. I don't see any point in making gardening complicated, when much of it is based on common sense and observation. (All the key techniques are explained and illustrated, and I've included plenty of tips and tricks of the trade.)

There are suggestions on the best plants and the best varieties to grow in particular situations and for a particular effect. I've tried to keep the information crisp and to the point so that you can find what you need quickly and easily and then put your new-found knowledge into practice. Don't worry if you're not familiar with the Latin names of plants. They are there to make sure you can find the plant as it will be labelled in the nursery or garden centre, but where appropriate I have included common names, too. Forgetting a plant's name need not stand in your way when it comes to being able to grow it.

Above all, the *How to Garden* books are designed to fill you with passion and enthusiasm for your garden and all that its creation and care entails, from designing and planting it to maintaining it and enjoying it. For more than fifty years gardening has been my passion, and that initial enthusiasm for watching plants grow, for trying something new and for just being outside pottering has never faded. If anything I am keener on gardening now than I ever was and get more satisfaction from my plants every day. It's not that I am simply a romantic, but rather that I have learned to look for the good in gardens and in plants, and there is lots to be found. Oh, there are times when I fail – when my plants don't grow as well as they should and I need to try harder. But where would I rather be on a sunny day? Nowhere!

The *How to Garden* handbooks will, I hope, allow some of that enthusiasm – childish though it may be – to rub off on you, and the information they contain will, I hope, make you a better gardener, as well as opening your eyes to the magic of plants and flowers.

Getting to know shade

Every garden has at least one patch of shade, and some gardens are in shadow for most of the time. All too often, these areas are neglected because they are considered difficult. Yet many plants actually prefer to spend some time in the shade, especially in summer when the sun can be relentless. Shade is an asset – so much so that if your garden has little or no shade it is well worth creating some. If your garden already has plenty, you can get going straight away – transforming that ivy-covered, moss-ridden corner into one of the most delightful and rewarding parts of your garden.

Types of shade

You don't need to be an expert gardener to recognize shade. Go outside on a sunny day and you will see it slicing up your garden into segments. But what type of shade are you looking at? And how much light actually gets to ground level where the plants grow? It is clear that not all shade is the same. The very fact that there are so many words to describe it – dappled, heavy, light, partial, full, temporary, permanent – is a good indication of its variety.

As a rule, east- and west-facing walls provide temporary shade.

Definitions and degrees

Apart from the wonderful dappled shade that you find under the canopies of deciduous trees – where filtered light makes shifting patterns on the woodland floor – there's the altogether more permanent, darker, shade found alongside evergreen hedges. There's temporary shade along east- and west-facing boundaries: the wall that greets the sunrise will be in full shade by the afternoon, while the west-facing wall, shaded in the morning, will be in full sun by the afternoon. There's amorphous shade, too, which hugs larger plants and garden structures and creeps and changes as the sun tracks its way across the sky.

Shade changes with the time of year. Borders adjacent to buildings in full sun in summer are plunged into near-continuous shade during the depths of winter, while areas protected from the summer's midday sun by deciduous trees are a whole lot lighter in winter when the trees have lost their leaves.

So what does all this mean for the gardener? First, it means the range of plants you can grow in your garden is dramatically increased. Specimens that are scorched by direct sunlight sigh with relief under the canopy of others.

Shade usually means shelter, too, where tender plants can nestle securely under the protection of more robust neighbours.

Not all seemingly shady corners are the same: those enjoying short periods of direct sun will give you scope for more varied plant displays.

Shady effects

In the softer light that shade affords, your eye can take in details denied to you in full sun. Suddenly you become aware of the subtle changes in tone in the petals of a flower, and wonder at the variety of foliage on display. Pale colours, which are so often bleached white in direct sun, are transformed into a palette of subtle pastels. On the other hand, darker tones, such as the purples that stand out so strongly in a sun-drenched spot, seem to melt into the background when viewed in the shadows.

Assessing shade

Before you can really make the most of shade-loving plants, you need to establish not only where the shady areas of your garden are, but what type of shade you are dealing with. Shady areas are categorized according to how much direct sunlight they get during the day, if any, as well as how dark they are when shaded.

In practical terms, shade can usually be defined as three main types: full (permanent), temporary (partial) and dappled.

To assess the extent and type of shade in your garden, carry out regular observations and record what you see. The best way to do this is to draw a sketch of your garden and mark on it the areas of shade at different times of the day, colour-coding the diagram perhaps,

or using tracing-paper overlays, so that you can see how different areas drift in and out of the shadows. Do the same thing in each season.

One way of gauging light levels in a garden is to use a light meter – as used by professional photographers.

Record how the areas of shade change in your garden as the sun tracks across the sky during the day. Repeat at different times of the year.

Note down which areas are affected by shade at ground level, and for how long. Try to gauge the depth of the shade, too.

Another is by personal observation. If, for example, you find difficulty reading in a shady area, chances are the light levels will be too low for most plants to thrive. On the other hand, if you can read comfortably then the amount of available light is likely to be pretty much ideal for most shade-loving plants. In situations where the white of the page is starting to glare, there should be enough light for plants liking only partial shade to do well.

As a general rule, the lower the sun gets in winter the lower the light levels are throughout the garden, and the areas of shade increase in size.

Don't forget

You can make the most of an area of permanent shade by creating a grotto using hardy ferns and other foliage shade-lovers (see page 31).

Full shade

Areas in permanent shade, such as those in the shadow of tall buildings or alongside the north side of walls and other garden structures, are often quite challenging. As well as receiving no sunlight, the soil here is usually very dry because building overhang prevents rain falling on the ground and foundations draw out the moisture from the soil by capillary action. With new-build properties, borders next to the house have invariably been used as a convenient dumping ground for rubble, sand and gravel, so the problems of dry soil are exacerbated and your choice of plants is therefore quite restricted.

The ground under evergreen shrubs also suffers from deep shade more often than not. Light levels here tend to be even lower than in the shadow of buildings and the soil is probably as dry (if not drier)

Borders close to buildings often have to cope with permanent shade, but with careful planting they can be just as attractive as any other.

due to the removal of moisture by the fibrous roots of trees and shrubs, which spread to the surface.

Temporary shade

Areas of temporary shade are created as the sun tracks across the sky through the day. East-facing walls and fences get early-morning sun but fall under the spell of deepening shadow as the sun moves round, bathing west-facing walls and fences in golden light by late afternoon.

These areas can be one of the best places to grow plants because they are guaranteed some sun yet have plenty of light at other times of the day. Here, try and choose plants that are recommended for

Where to find the shady spots

TYPE OF SHADE	SITUATION
Temporary shade (partial shade): sunlight in the morning or evening but shaded at midday	East- or west-facing areas of the garden next to boundary walls and fences, as well as areas next to large shrubs or hedges
Dappled shade (light shade): shaded all day, but with flickering sunlight	Under the canopy of deciduous trees, for example
Full shade (deep shade, permanent shade): permanent shade with no direct sunlight	Between buildings or close to north-facing walls and fences, and under evergreen hedges

In high summer, areas of partial or dappled shade areas are a delight – and there are plenty of shrubs and perennials that will thrive in these conditions.

use in 'sun' or 'partial shade', such as *Ajuga reptans* (bugle), *Alchemilla mollis* (lady's mantle), *Anemone* x *hybrida*, bergenia (elephant's ears), *Actaea racemosa* (bugbane), *Dicentra spectabilis* (bleeding heart) and *Choisya ternata* (Mexican orange blossom).

Temporary shade can also be seasonal in nature, such as in deciduous woodland in summer. Native plants are well adapted to making the most of the early-spring sunlight that filters through the tracery of twigs high above before the canopy of new foliage emerges. You can take advantage of these early-emerging bulbs and perennials to cover the ground under deciduous shrubs and trees in your garden.

Many shade-tolerant, spring-flowering bulbs are useful here too.

For example, try planting sparkling clusters of *Anemone blanda,* or erythroniums set off by an evergreen sward of ivy. Combine them with colchicum and you'll get a colourful finale when the leaves fall in autumn. Bear in mind though that some deciduous trees, such as beech, form a particularly dense canopy, which makes planting under them rather less successful.

Dappled shade

Lightly shaded areas that remain partially shaded at all times are less common, especially in small gardens. They are the woodland-edge or glade-style gardens that can look stunning planted with shade-tolerant bulbs and perennials. As it is relatively light, it is easy to forget that dappled shade is constant shade, so plants needing the full strength of the sun to flower often under-perform in these areas. Choose those recommended for 'partial shade'.

Don't forget

The distinction between dry shade and moist shade is an important one and plants should be chosen accordingly.

Cyclamen coum copes well with the dry soil caused by the roots of silver birch. Although here the bulbs are in flower before the dancing leaves of the trees break through, they can easily tolerate dappled and partial shade.

Adaptations to the shadows

In order to survive in a whole range of habitats, climates and conditions, plants have had to evolve in different ways to make the most of the resources available. Shade-lovers are no exception.

Plant characteristics

All plants need light, so in shady areas a plant's ability to grow is restricted: the darker the shade, the slower the growth. To overcome this, shade-tolerant plants have developed various characteristics to enable them to photosynthesize as efficiently as possible.

Plants that grow best in shade and make the most of low-light conditions tend to have a thin surface layer and large, flat leaves, allowing maximum light to reach the chloroplasts (*see* box).

Another characteristic is that their leaves are generally smooth, so there is nothing to impede the light penetrating the leaf surface. The arrangement of leaves on shade-tolerant plants often differs to those of their sun-loving cousins, too. As a rule, plants that thrive in the shadows hold their leaves out at right-angles to the stem to maximize the amount of light that falls on them. Contrast this with sun-worshippers, such as yucca and phormium, which keep their leaves pointing upwards at about 45 degrees to limit their exposure to the rays.

Darker-coloured leaves help many shade-lovers absorb the sun's energy more efficiently, whereas many sun-loving plants, such as euphorbias and verbascums, have pale-coloured foliage to help reflect some of the light.

Often, shade-lovers also have long stems between leaf joints to allow them to reach up to the light, while their roots tend to be shallow to take advantage of the nutrients released by decomposing leaf litter.

Efficient use of energy

As a rule, well-adapted shade plants are slower-growing than sun-lovers, making them less competitive when they are planted in full sun.

To make the best use of restricted light resources, they also tend to produce a profusion of energy-gathering leaves and stems rather than flowers and seeds, with the result that many garden shade-lovers are known for their spectacular ornamental foliage rather than colour.

Wildflowers that grow in deciduous woodland make maximum use of available light. Bluebells, for example, grow before the leaves on most trees start to break, and flower while there is still plenty of light filtering through.

The thin surface layer of many shade-adapted plants means they will burn if subjected to prolonged, hot sun.

Shady situations

Most gardens have several areas of shade, often with a range of conditions. Since plants vary in their ability to grow in different types of shade, it is important to choose varieties for each situation with care.

Planting under trees

The light, dappled shade found under deciduous trees is perhaps the most alluring of shady areas and can be a delight when planted with colourful drifts of perennials and bulbs that provide an ever-changing tapestry of colour through the seasons. However, some trees are more generous than others with their light, so take this into account when designing the display. For example, beech trees have such a dense canopy of foliage that most perennials and bulbs struggle to survive underneath. Here, choose plants such as snowdrops and wood anemones, which produce their leaves and flowers early, before the trees leaf-up fully. By the time the beech canopy fills out and dramatically reduces light levels the plants have died back and are unaffected.

Some trees, such as birch, may seem to allow plenty of light down to ground level but produce masses of fibrous surface roots that dry out the soil and rob it of nutrients, so understorey plants struggle to get established. One solution in these circmstances is to cut out planting holes and line them with old, untreated timber to give the new plants time to establish before roots from the surrounding trees invade.

Moist and dry shade

In shady areas, the moisture level around the roots will dictate which plants you can grow. Moist shade is common on heavy soils with poor drainage, or where the shade is cast at the bottom of a slope.

Areas of shade with dry soil often occur next to buildings and walls, as well as beside shallow-rooted larger plants. Anything you plant in dry shade will need watering regularly until well established and an annual spring mulch of well-rotted organic matter will help to conserve moisture in the soil.

Problem areas

Evergreen trees are particularly difficult to plant under because they cast deep shade all year round. Since the soil is often dry too, it's more important than ever to choose plants that can cope with such conditions.

Good shrubs to try in these dry, shady areas include varieties of *Aucuba japonica*, *Berberidopsis corallina*, camellia, *Danae racemosa*, *Euonymus fortunei* and *Fatsia japonica*.

Suitable herbaceous perennials include varieties of *Ajuga reptans*, lily-of-the-valley, *Epimedium perralderianum*, *Liriope muscari*, *Lysimachia nummularia* and *Pulmonaria saccharata* (lungwort).

Where areas are shaded by coniferous trees, such as spruce or pines, decomposing pine needles are an additional problem as they make the soil too acid for most plants to survive.

When planting a display beneath deciduous trees, be sure to take into account the varying soil and light conditions they dictate.

In a north-facing border against a boundary fence you will need to choose plants, such as hardy ferns, that can cope with the permanent shade.

Alongside walls and garden boundaries

The light levels at the base of a vertical structure such as a wall or fence will largely depend on the direction it is facing, as well as the nature of the established plants nearby. Against a north wall there is invariably an area that lies in permanent shade all year round, although this may be reduced in scope and severity when the sun is high in the sky during early summer. East- and west-facing walls and fences normally get at least some direct sunlight either early in the morning or during late afternoon.

As with house walls (*see* Full shade, page 11), the soil next to boundary walls and fences tends to be dry. Just how dry depends on both the direction of the prevailing winds and the soil type. This effect is exacerbated near a warm, sunny wall as it acts as a night-storage radiator, increasing evaporation of moisture from the surrounding soil. However, here you can grow more tender plants than might otherwise be able to survive in your garden. Conversely, solid boundaries across slopes can trap cold winter air, creating frost pockets that will limit your choice (*see also* Focus on microclimates, page 17).

Don't forget

Some plants, notably camellias, are damaged by rapid thawing after a frost so avoid planting them where they catch the early-morning sunlight.

Between buildings

Plants are invaluable between buildings, softening the edges of hard landscaping and providing a visual and textural contrast to masonry and glass. Unfortunately, this is quite a difficult area in which to grow plants successfully because

as well as low light levels and dry soil, there may be buffeting currents of air. This increases transpiration and in windy weather causes physical damage. In very gusty locations it is as well to put up a temporary windbreak until the plants find their feet.

For these dry, shady, windy conditions try box, pachysandra, *Prunus laurocerasus* 'Otto Luyken', *Ruscus aculeatus* (butcher's broom), sarcococca, symphoricarpos, holly, hypericum or mahonia, under-planted with periwinkle, lily-of-the-valley, *Euphorbia amygdaloides* var. *robbiae* and *Iris foetidissima*, with various ivies or a climbing hydrangea covering the walls. However, even these will need extra care to get them established.

Ivies can usually be relied on to grow where all else fails: there are few spots that will defeat them, even deep shade.

Skirting shrubs

Ground-cover plants and bulbs are a great way to set off specimen shrubs and for filling the gaps between shrubs in a border. Often these areas get at least some direct sunlight as the sun moves around the sky during the day, so you can grow a good range of plants. The main limiting factors here are competition from the established shrubs and the space available.

A good solution is to choose low-growing carpeting perennials (such as ajuga, lamium and pulmonaria), mixed with bulbs to provide seasonal colour and interest.

Another option is to include a climber or two, which can be allowed to scramble through larger shrubs. Clematis, in particular, thrive in this situation because they like to have their roots in the cool of shade with their tops in the sun.

Under shady windows choose drought-tolerant, low-maintenance plants that do not need regular cutting back.

Shady borders below windows

These areas can be tricky if you are to maintain an unrestricted view and not have plants interfering with the opening and closing of the windows. As with other borders next to walls, the soil is likely to be dry and impoverished. It is therefore essential to improve it before planting by removing any debris and incorporating plenty of well-rotted organic matter.

In a front garden, suitable plants include *Euonymus fortunei* 'Emerald 'n' Gold', an evergreen with yellow-edged leaves that become pink-tinged in winter, or shrubby *Hebe rakaiensis*, which makes neat cushions of glossy, fresh-green leaves topped by frothy spikes of small white flowers in early summer.

Combine these with equally tolerant perennials, such as *Alchemilla mollis* (lady's mantle), which forms mounds of scalloped foliage and a frothy haze of tiny yellow flowers in summer, and *Liriope muscari* (blue lily-turf), with its fountains of dark-green strappy leaves highlighted by long-lasting, vibrant wands of deep-violet flowers during late summer.

Borders with shrubs need shade-tolerant plants that will provide year-round interest or come into their own before or after the shrubs are at their best.

The growing conditions in any garden will vary between one area and another, depending on a number of factors. The most important of these is where you live – such as how far north and how high above sea level.

Local climate

Local factors play their part too. The climate in a city, for example, is completely different from the climate in a rural area because the heat leaking out of the buildings warms the air to create a milder microclimate: plants that would succumb to the first frost in country areas can grow through the winter quite happily in sheltered urban locations.

If you live by the sea, your garden will be less cold in winter than its inland equivalent. The large body of water acts like a giant night-storage heater, keeping coastal areas a few degrees warmer at night.

In the garden

Areas of microclimate can be tiny. For example, in a natural dip or hollow, where cold air will naturally collect, frosts will be more severe. Solid barriers such as walls or fences in a sloping garden can have the same effect – trapping the cold, sinking air to create a frost pocket. On a cold,

sunny morning check whether there are any areas where the frost lingers after the rest of the garden has thawed. On the other hand, if the garden is exposed to wind, then a hollow may provide a degree of shelter not offered elsewhere in the garden.

Rainfall may be significantly less in some shaded areas, such as in the lee of walls and fences. The extent of the rain shadow will be determined by both the height of the structure and the normal strength of the prevailing wind.

You can exploit the microclimates in your garden to grow a greater range of plants, or introduce features specifically to create them. For example, build a raised bed with a slight south-facing slope to the surface to make the most of any available sunlight.

Take advantage of microclimates in a garden to create interest all year round. ① In a sheltered corner you have a good choice of plants, including borderline-hardy varieties and those averse to wind. ② Even a frost pocket can be turned to advantage by planting frost-hardy evergreens such as this hellebore.

Microclimates at a glance

Under deciduous trees and shrubs
- Dappled shade
- Dry soil
- Sheltered from wind
- Sheltered from frost

Under evergreen trees
- Continuous shade
- Dry soil
- Sheltered from wind
- Sheltered from frost

East-facing boundary wall
- Temporary shade (evenings)
- May be dry soil
- May be a frost pocket
- May be buffeted by cold winds

West-facing boundary wall
- Temporary shade (mornings)
- May be dry soil
- May be a frost pocket
- May be buffeted by winds

North-facing boundary wall
- Continuous shade
- May be dry soil
- May be a frost pocket
- May be buffeted by cold winds

Between buildings
- Continuous shade
- May be very dry soil
- Wind tunnel
- May be sheltered from frost

Creating shade

Lack of shade can be as much of a drawback as too much in terms of enjoyment of the garden in summer and the range of plants you can grow. Fortunately, there are several things you can do to create shade – from planting trees to installing garden features.

Hedges not only provide security, shelter, privacy and an attractive backdrop to borders, they can also be used to create ribbons of shade.

Trees

Planting a tree is a relatively long-term solution and it is important to bear in mind the effect it will have on nearby building foundations. Well-behaved trees such as *Malus* 'Red Jade' (flowering crab apple) or *Prunus* 'Kiku-shidare-zakura' (flowering cherry) can be planted about 4m (13ft) from a house, while most small garden trees, such as *Gleditsia triacanthos* 'Sunburst', *Sorbus* 'Joseph Rock' and the silver birch *Betula utilis* var. *jacquemontii*, need a 10m (32ft) gap. Larger garden trees such as *Robinia pseudoacacia*, *Liquidambar styraciflua* and *Fagus sylvatica* 'Purpurea' should be given at least 12m (40ft). *See* pages 115–18 for a selection of other trees suitable for small- to medium-sized gardens.

Hedges

Fast-growing hedges are useful for providing shade. It's best to avoid the ubiquitous × *Cupressocyparis leylandii* (Leyland cypress) though because it can reach 30m (100ft) or more and may need trimming twice a year (once in mid-spring and once in summer) to keep it in check. The golden variety 'Castlewellan' is a preferable option because it grows at about half the speed. Or be creative and grow a living wall of vigorous bamboo instead.

Hedges to consider (approximate heights are at five years):

Carpinus betulus (hornbeam): deciduous, but retains its brown leaves in winter. H 1.8m (6ft)

Chamaecyparis lawsoniana (Lawson cypress): evergreen. H 2m (6ft)

Crataegus monogyna (hawthorn): deciduous and thorny. H 1.5m (5ft)

Fagus sylvatica (beech): deciduous, but retains its brown leaves in winter. H 1.8m (6ft)

Ligustrum ovalifolium (privet): evergreen. H 1.5m (5ft)

Prunus lusitanica (Portugal laurel): evergreen. H 1.8m (6ft)

Thuja plicata (western red cedar): evergreen. H 2m (6ft)

Planting a small tree will provide both a focal point to the garden and, given time, welcome dappled shade.

Arches

In a small garden arches can be a useful way of providing shade over a seat. Plant them with fragrant climbers such as the woodbine honeysuckles *Lonicera periclymenum* 'Belgica' (reddish-purple and yellow flowers) or 'Serotina' (reddish-purple and white flowers). Together these climbers will provide a succession of colour and scent, as the former flowers mainly during early summer and the latter during late summer.

Lonicera x *heckrottii* (yellow and purple flowers) is a better choice if the seat is likely to be used most on evenings later in the season, since this honeysuckle is particularly noted for its evening fragrance from midsummer onwards.

As well as creating lovely shady walkways, arches can be used singly as a gateway to another part of the garden or as a point of interest.

Arches can also provide a feature or focal point in a garden (*see* page 30). If there is space, you could set up a series: space them 2–3m (6–10ft) apart. Bear in mind that as the climbers grow they will reduce both the height and the width of an arch, which in practice means it should be at least 1.2m (4ft) wide and well over 2m (6ft) high.

Style and construction

There are two main types of arch, formal and informal, both of which can be bought in kit form in a variety of materials. Formal arches are available in wood, metal or plastic, while informal types are usually of rustic-wood construction. As a rule, metal arches are easier to handle and put up because they slot together neatly and come with pre drilled holes and bolts. Wooden arches are more variable, usually depending on the quality and the price. They tend to be more difficult to put together and pre-drilled holes and slots aren't always accurately located.

Whatever type of arch you choose, it will need to be positioned carefully so that it is vertical and square. Check this with a spirit-level.

Garden structures can be used to provide relief from the sun in a south-facing garden: once they are clad in sun-worshipping climbers, choose shade-lovers to create a display below.

All arches must be well anchored, preferably in concrete footings. They will need to be robust enough to bear the weight of a vigorous climber or two in full leaf, which in high winds will also act like a sail.

Pergolas

Traditionally, pergolas are built of wood, perhaps with brick pillars supporting the timbers overhead. Proprietary pergolas are heavy to handle and require at least two pairs of hands to put together. You may need two pairs of steps too, as holding heavy timbers above head height while they are being fitted is tiring!

Uses and position

As pergolas are larger and more substantial structures than arches they offer more possibilities for providing shade. Use them next to the house on a sunny patio to create seating areas for eating out and entertaining, or position one in the middle of the garden as a dramatic focal point and an access hub to all other parts of the garden. Placed further down the garden, partially hidden from view, a pergola becomes a shady sanctuary.

A patio pergola can be a freestanding structure or lean-to construction. Try to balance its size with the area so it doesn't dominate. Make sure too that the roof timbers are far enough off the ground so that any scrambling climbers are well above head height.

It's a good idea to avoid overhead climbers that are susceptible to aphids, otherwise the seating area may become unusable during the summer months when the insects drip sticky honeydew as they feed. Steer clear of honeysuckles for this reason, and restrict roses to the posts.

Don't forget

You don't have to restrict your choice of climbers to ornamental varieties. Some cane fruits and briars can be trained over an arch or pergola. Choose prickle-free varieties such as thornless boysenberry, or the blackberries 'Oregon Thornless' or 'Smoothstem'. On a pergola, try a fruiting grape vine, such as *Vitis* 'Brant', which has leaves that turn bronze-red in autumn and produces edible, blue-black grapes.

Shade sails and awnings

These are an ideal way of creating instant shade in and around the garden. Awnings are like giant rollerblinds that fix to the outside wall of the house (usually over the patio doors) and can be pulled out on a hot sunny day to provide immediate protection from the

Sometimes it's good to be able to have instant shade wherever you want it – but make sure that sail-like awnings are easily removable should a breeze get up.

searing sunlight. Although expensive to buy, they do provide the ultimate in convenience and can be rolled away when normal British summer weather resumes.

Awnings also allow you to extend your living area into the garden and create a more intimate atmosphere for eating al fresco on the patio, without risk of the occasion being spoilt by an untimely summer shower.

Shade sails, on the other hand, are altogether more versatile and can be fixed to walls, trees, fence posts or any other sturdy structure. They can be strung up anywhere in the garden, such as on patios or over play areas, or packed up in the car to provide shade and shower protection wherever and whenever you want.

Climbers for arches and pergolas

You can combine two or more climbers on an arch, either training one up each side or intermingling them to extend the flowering season and add more impact. With combinations, aim to match the vigour and cultural requirements of the plants, such as pruning, so they are easier to look after. Pergolas can support larger climbers such as wisteria and more vigorous roses, or perhaps a vine.

Near-thornless varieties of climbing rose include 'Handel' (double cream-edged pink flowers), 'Kathleen Harrop' (double pale-pink flowers) or 'Zéphirine Drouhin' (semi-double carmine-pink flowers).

To add fragrance, grow scented climbing roses such as 'Albéric Barbier' (double creamy-lemon flowers), 'Albertine'

(double pale-pink flowers), 'Swan Lake' (double pink-flushed white flowers) or 'Emily Gray' (double yellow flowers). *Jasminum officinale* (common white jasmine), with its white late-summer flowers, or *J. beesianum*, with its pinkish-red early-summer blooms, are both good for scent, too.

If you are planting clematis, place them on the north side so that their roots are cool. Where this is not possible, plant shade-providing shrubs or cover the ground with large pebbles to achieve the same effect. Try *Clematis alpina*, *C. armandii* or *C. macropetala* for spring flowers, followed in early summer by *C. montana* varieties and early-flowering hybrid clematis.

For year-round interest, try an evergreen climber such as *Hedera colchica* 'Dentata Variegata' (Persian ivy). *See also pages 94–8.*

Quick summer cover-ups

For a while, until the perennial climbers have grown up and over a new structure to soften its outline, a new arch or pergola can look a bit stark. To overcome this, consider planting quick-growing annual climbers to help integrate it into its garden setting within the first year. Most annual climbers will grow 3m (10ft) or more, so can soon look really effective. To make the most of tender annuals, start them off in pots under cover.

Cobaea scandens (not illustrated)
(Cup and saucer vine)

Large, bell-shaped flowers open yellowish green and age to purple. Each flower sits on a large, flat, green leafy calyx that looks like a saucer – hence its common name. During late winter or early spring soak seed for 24 hours before sowing individually in cellular trays and place in a propagator maintained at 18°C (65°F). Plant out after last frosts.

① *Eccremocarpus scaber*
(Chilean glory flower)

Exotic-looking spikes of orange-tipped red flowers. Sow in late winter or early spring in cellular trays and place in a propagator maintained at 13°C (55°F). Plant out after last frosts.

② *Lathyrus odoratus*
(Sweet pea)

Highly fragrant blooms on long stems in a range of delicious colours. During early autumn or early spring, soak seed for 24 hours on a moist kitchen towel, sowing individually in cellular trays. Maintain a temperature of 4°C (40°F). Plant out as soon as soil and weather conditions permit.

③ *Thunbergia alata*
(Black-eyed Susan)

Cream, yellow or orange flat-petalled flowers with a striking chocolate-brown centre.

In early to mid-spring, soak seed for 24 hours before sowing individually in cellular trays and germinate at a temperature of 21°C (70°F). Plant out after last frosts.

④ *Ipomoea tricolor*
(Morning glory)

Large, trumpet-shaped flowers in shades of purple, pink, red and blue. Sow several seeds to a small pot in late winter or early spring and germinate at a temperature of 21°C (70°F). Thin out to leave the strongest seedlings after germination. Plant out after last frosts.

Tropaeolum peregrinum (not illustrated)
(Canary creeper)

Clusters of small butter-yellow flowers over a dense covering of bright-green, lobed leaves. Sow several seeds to a small pot during early spring and germinate at a temperature of 21°C (70°F). Thin out to leave the strongest seedlings after germination. Plant out after last frosts.

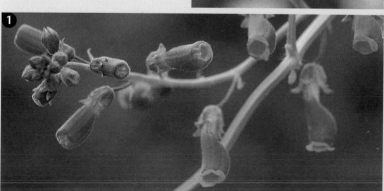

Creating light

You can improve the light levels in nearly all shady gardens by making adjustments to nearby plantings and maximizing opportunities to open up areas. Light-enhancing design features and understorey plants play their part, too.

Tackling trees

In theory, any tree in your garden can be pruned to open up the canopy to allow more light to reach the area beneath (once all the relevant permissions have been sought, *see* Don't forget, below). However, this is easier said than done, so it is best to get help and advice from a reputable tree surgeon in your area at the outset. The careless pruning of trees not only spoils their appearance, but can weaken or unbalance them – making them vulnerable to strong winds – and may encourage serious rots and other problems to gain a hold. Remember that tree pruning will need to be repeated periodically as the tree puts on replacement growth.

Don't forget

Before you start pruning trees, whether they be on your own property or on someone else's, you must contact your local authority planning department to find out whether the tree is protected by a TPO (Tree Preservation Order). If it is, you will need to apply for permission for the work to be done, which may take several months. Failure to do so could result in a substantial fine, even if you were unaware that the tree was covered by a TPO. In conservation areas trees may be further protected. Always consult with your neighbours before doing any work on their trees, and if you are renting the property seek the permission of the owner.

There are four main methods of tree pruning: crown lifting, crown reduction, crown thinning and crown removal (pollarding).

Crown lifting This is an artificial way of increasing the space under a tree by removing its lowest branches. It effectively reduces the depth of the crown, allowing more light to penetrate through the canopy to ground level. Crown lifting is the easiest pruning technique to master, as identifying which branches to remove and

Here, the airy, open canopy of *Robinia pseudoacacia* 'Frisia' causes less of a shade problem than the dense foliage of the larger tree behind it, which would almost certainly require professional pruning.

where to cut is very straightforward and you may not even have to leave the ground to do the work. The technique is useful for trees next to paths and driveways, overhanging seating areas, or where a tree is restricting the view.

Crown reduction
With this method, the tree canopy is given a short-back-and-sides, reducing its overall size proportionally. The symmetry and balance of the tree should not be affected. This is a useful technique for trees growing too close to buildings or those whose branches are interfering with overhead cables. Although it doesn't require too much skill, it is the most difficult pruning method to achieve because you have to get to the end of every branch.

Crown thinning
This reduces the density of the crown by strategically removing a proportion of the branches so that the overall shape and balance of the tree is left unaffected. Reducing the density of the crown allows more light through, brightening up the area underneath. Although the cuts are easier to make, the process requires a great deal of skill and experience to get right. This method works well with old trees that need old or damaged branches removed, as well as on exposed sites where a tree is being damaged by strong winds. Crown thinning effectively reduces a tree's wind resistance and so makes it more stable when seasonal gales blow.

Crown removal (pollarding)
Some trees, including horse chestnuts, limes, planes and willows, will respond to even more severe pruning. Known as pollarding, the technique is often employed in urban areas to keep street trees within bounds. Here, the whole crown is cut back to a few stubby branches. These then throw up new, vigorous shoots to create a lollipop-shaped tree. Every few years this process can be repeated. Pollarding reduces the shade of a tree dramatically, so permanent plants underneath have to be able to cope with a sudden deluge of direct sun as well as increasing amounts of dappled shade as the tree's branches grow.

Increase the light levels under trees by pruning the canopy. Which method you use will depend on the type of tree and the finished effect you are trying to achieve.

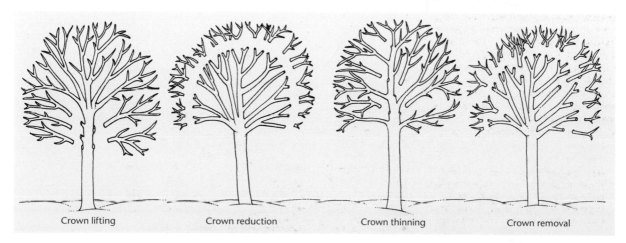

Crown lifting   Crown reduction   Crown thinning   Crown removal

Stand under a tree on a sunny day (preferably at two or three different times) and look up to gauge what effect pruning the canopy might have.

Neighbours' trees

It's probably safe to say that half of all shade cast by trees is caused by trees in neighbouring gardens. In the UK there is no legal 'right to light', so if a neighbour's tree shades your garden there is very little you can do about it. The best solution is to talk to your neighbour about your concerns to see if you can come to an amicable arrangement. Maybe offer to pay for the work if that is a possibility. If this does not prove successful, you do have the right to remove all branches that overhang your garden at the point where they cross the boundary. However, you must offer to return all the bits you cut off, otherwise you could be accused of stealing. *See also* Don't forget, page 22.

Creating pools of light

You can transform the appearance of a shady garden by creating a sunny island and planting it with shade-tolerant specimens. Go out on a sunny day and see where different tree or shrub canopies meet. If the foliage cover is quite sparse, open it up by carefully pruning back each of the overhanging trees or shrubs to create sunny glades at ground level. Bear in mind that any pruning will stimulate new growth, so you will have to prune the overhang regularly to maintain

HOW TO remove a tree limb

When removing large branches do so in stages to avoid the weight of the branch ripping away and damaging the tree trunk.

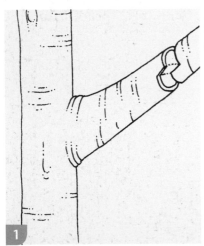

1 Make the first cut *underneath* the branch being removed, 30–45cm (12–18in) away from the trunk. It is vital not to cut all the way through. Then make a second cut in the top of the branch, a few centimetres further away from the trunk.

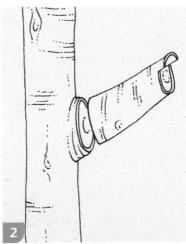

2 The bulk of the branch should then fall away, leaving a stump. This can be removed by making a third cut close to the trunk. Take care to leave the collar (ridge of bark where the branch joins the trunk), as this will help the wound to heal and reduce the chances of infection. Special wound-sealant paint is available, but it is unclear how beneficial this is.

the opening. Before planting, observe the effect of the sun on your new sunspot as it moves round from east to west.

Controlling shrubs

It often becomes apparent only after the offending plants are cut back or removed just how much light overgrown shrubs and hedges cut out, particularly if they are evergreen. The benefit of pruning overgrown shrubs is twofold: not only will it open up the surrounding area, but it will also improve the overall appearance and performance of the shrub. The new, vigorous growth will have better foliage colour and, on flowering shrubs, a larger and more prolific display.

Different shrubs favour different pruning methods, so check which one your shrub likes before you start. Some, including dogwoods, respond well to being cut right back to a short, stubby framework near to the ground. They then willingly throw up new, vigorous shoots from just above or just below soil level.

Others, however, will not appreciate such harsh treatment. Here, use the more cautious technique of cutting out one in three stems, starting with the oldest. New growth will shoot up to replace the old. Repeat this process three years running and

you will have rejuvenated the whole shrub with new growth. This is the best option to use for shrubs you cannot identify.

Reducing hedges

Old, overgrown and neglected hedges can be reduced in size, but only if they are of a type that responds to drastic pruning, such as yew, privet, hawthorn and beech. Severe pruning is best carried out during the winter months when the hedge is dormant.

Visualizing the final shape of a hedge when you are pruning away a lot of foliage material can be difficult, so make a profile of the outline you are trying to achieve by using pieces of old timber.

Stand this alongside the hedge periodically to make sure you do not cut away too much. The easiest method is to cut one end of the hedge to the right shape, then move the profile along as you cut. Trim the hedge slightly narrower and shorter than the eventual height you want so that the new growth can be trimmed to the desired height and you won't have to cut into older stems again.

Some conifer hedges can be difficult to prune severely because they are reluctant to resprout new growth if you cut into old wood (*see* Pruning conifers, page 54).

Sometimes a hedge needs to be removed completely. This can be very, very hard work – many a

Most overgrown hedges can be pruned to let in more light. One way to ensure a good line is to use a pair of canes and taut string as a guide when cutting.

spade handle has been broken in the course of hacking out old stumps. Where practicable, hire a winch that can be anchored to something immovable, such as a tree, to do a lot of the hard work for you. Once the stump has been loosened you will be able to see where the remaining roots are and these can be chopped through with an axe, pruning saw or grubbing mattock until the stump is freed completely. Another option is to hire a stump grinder or chipper that chips away the woody part, leaving smaller roots in the ground.

Minimizing boundaries

In a north-facing garden, high boundary walls and fences can cast a shadow over almost all the garden not affected by the house itself. You can overcome this to some extent by making the boundaries more open – for example, by removing 1.8m (6ft) fence panels and replacing them with 1.2m (4ft) panels topped with

Open fences will let more light and air into the garden than solid boundaries, and when clad with climbers there is no loss of privacy.

60cm (2ft) of trellis. Once decorated with climbers, the garden will appear to be lighter and bigger. Another option is to stain large panels with a

pale shade of preservative to help reflect the available light back into the garden, or plant variegated ivies and other light-reflecting climbers to clothe the panels in foliage, which will achieve a similar effect.

Paving and walls

In shady courtyards or between buildings the choice of paving is key: it is essential that it is in keeping with the materials used for the walls, but choose a paler shade if possible, which will help reflect the available light. You can help break up large areas of paving by combining two or more complementary materials to create patterns or zones. Pebbles, gravel and stone chippings are all worth considering, so too are coloured glass chippings for a more

Make the most of light colours to alleviate shade. Here, bright foliage and pale-coloured pebbles and stones help maximize the available light.

It's all done with mirrors

Introducing mirrors designed to resemble gates or windows is a useful design trick for creating light and the illusion of space. Make sure the mirror is angled to reflect a pleasant view, but avoid positioning it where it reflects a sunny area as this will produce a counter-effective glare.

To make the whole illusion more convincing, frame the mirror with climbers or a mock archway of clipped bay. A similar effect can be achieved at a fraction of the cost using small-leaved ivies trained over columns of stiff green plastic mesh. With mirrors designed to look like garden gates, create a meandering path of cobbles or gravel to lead the eye towards it.

Reflective surfaces can also be used to create the illusion of a gap in a hedge or wall. Hide the edges of the mirror with foliage and make it all the more intriguing by planting a see-through plant in front, such as long-stemmed bamboo.

Mirrors can be used effectively on the ground, too. You can create a crystal pool in a ferny grotto, or a mock stream running though shade-loving perennials. Hide all the edges of the mirror from view for best effect.

with a mirror in the central panel to increase the sense of space and light. Mirrored faux window frames complete with planted window boxes are also available.

Walls can be painted too. Pale creams, light beiges and greys are better than white, because they look less stark. Choose a special masonry paint that won't need reapplying every year.

If you want to grow climbers up the painted walls it's a good idea to make sure the supporting trellis is hinged so that it is easy to swing the top-growth of the climber away from the wall during maintenance. Or choose climbers that can be cut back to ground level, such as *Clematis* 'Abundance', 'Bill MacKenzie', 'Duchess of Albany', 'Etoile Violette', 'Jackmanii', 'Perle d'Azur' and 'Ville de Lyon' (all pruning group 3, *see* page 54).

contemporary finish. Add artificial rills using strips of mirror set below gullies created between runs of flagstones to complete the look and bring a sparkle to gloomy corridors as they reflect the sky above (*see* page 37).

The walls of buildings can be broken up with collections of wall containers and hanging baskets filled with variegated foliage plants and pale-coloured flowers. Another option is to use perspective trellis

For boundary or retaining walls in shady sites, use light-reflecting natural materials such as this pale grey slate to give the area a lift.

Designing with shade

The key to success with any garden design is to take advantage of the conditions by selecting the right plants and combining them to create effective displays. With shade, the same principles apply: don't go into battle with it; instead make the most of what you've got in the way of natural features, and introduce elements of surprise and interest. Some would say that design is primarily about making a statement – and that's surprisingly easy to do when it comes to planting in shade.

Celebrating foliage

To make the most of a shady area you need to think about designing with plants a little differently. Here, foliage is king – all else, including the most flamboyant of blooms, is secondary. Form and contrast are all-important. Take advantage of different plant forms to create structure within the scheme.

Emphasize an elegant fountain shape, for example, by planting contrasting rounded or low-growing plants alongside it. Choose bedfellows with dramatically different foliage, such as the lacy fronds of hardy ferns and the clean lines and simple shape of hosta leaves. Hostas also look fantastic when planted under the feathery, ornamental foliage of cut-leaf Japanese maples, making both plants the point of focus. Also consider the plant's natural 'footprint' – would it look most effective growing in clumps or swathes, or as a single specimen?

Creating atmosphere

Foliage can contribute to the atmosphere you want to create. Giant-leaved rodgersia and gunnera will instantly give a sense of the jungle, especially when reinforced by the tropical foliage of banana plants, arum lilies and tree ferns. On the other hand, ice-blue hostas planted alongside the fresh-green foliage of evergreen ferns or the yellow, grassy leaves of *Carex elata* 'Aurea' look most effective bordering deep, cool water, creating a sense of tranquillity.

Colour and contrast

Make the most of light-coloured foliage too. Not only will pale shades have an uplifting effect on gloomy areas, they will increase the amount of available light. Pale greens, iridescent blues and honey yellows all look great in shade. Here again you can add drama and interest by juxtaposing opposites, with banks of light alongside contrasting blocks of dark. It's worth taking into account that what looks dark in sunlight will appear jet-black in shade (*see* page 47).

It may be tempting to include a lot of variegated foliage plants in your shady display, but be cautious. Too much striking variegation can be hard on the eye. One option is to surround the high-tempo variegated

A shady border created solely from foliage and toning flowering plants can be just as dramatic as the most colourful herbaceous bed in full sun.

Don't forget

In a small garden, you can take advantage of the way the eye perceives textures and colours differently. Plants with bold and distinctive leaves, such as aucuba and bergenia, will seem closer than those with fine-textured or tiny leaves, such as box and cotoneaster. So a fence at the bottom of a garden covered with the plate-sized leaves of Virginia creeper, for example, will make the garden seem shorter than one fenced with a small-leaved ivy.

Shades of green: by combining foliage of varying tones, shapes and textures, highlighted by a flash of variegation, you can create a scheme that never seems dull.

colours with a cool pool of plain green as a visual antidote. Two or three contrasts in a combination are generally enough, otherwise the effect will be too fussy.

Many variegated plants lose their variegation in shade anyway, so that much of the benefit will be lost. The main exceptions are white- and silver-variegated plants, such as *Lamium maculatum* 'White Nancy' and variegated ivies, which maintain their light-reflecting splashes in even the darkest spots.

Leaves also vary in lustre. The high-gloss foliage of plants like fatsia is great for reflecting the available light into dingy corners. Foliage that bounces the light in this way is useful for adding depth to a scheme in shade, sparkling like diamonds in the darkest recesses.

Natural features

Many shady areas lend themselves to rustic-looking paths and steps: meandering paths made from wood chips or pulverized bark blend in perfectly. For something more permanent, consider recycled bricks or old flagstones made from limestone or sandstone, which will weather quickly and naturally. Gravel can be used too, if you don't mind it being colonized by moss or the self-sown seedlings of shade-loving annuals and perennials. Steps can be made from sawn logs or old railway sleepers, leaving gaps for ground-cover plants to soften the edges.

Take advantage of any variations in the natural landscape. Shady slopes and banks can be incorporated into the scheme to give it a natural sense of order, and by planting swathes of shade-tolerant perennials and bulbs you

Grouping plants

One way of seeing how plants will look together is to go down to your local garden centre and wheel around one of their jumbo trolleys, picking up shade-tolerant plants as you go. Find a shady spot and then juggle the trolley contents until you get something that seems to work. Bear in mind that all the plants you have chosen will look good at the same time, so include a balance of evergreen and deciduous plants, leaving mental gaps in the display so you can add earlier- or later-performing plants to extend the period of interest.

Building shallow steps and edging them with low-growing plants (*see* box, page 30) can turn a nondescript shady slope or pathway into something altogether more interesting.

Paths running through shady areas can be enhanced with complementary planting. Choose low-growing plants that don't produce unruly stems to trip you up.

In moisture-retentive soil you could try *Arum italicum* subsp. *italicum* 'Marmoratum' (lords and ladies). Its eye-catching, cream-veined arrow-shaped leaves provide ground cover from winter to late spring, followed by spikes of bright-orange berries.

In a well-drained spot try *Epimedium × rubrum* or *Epimedium × youngianum* 'Niveum', which form a carpet of bronze-tinted leaves and carry airy sprays of flowers during late spring.

Focal points

A specimen tree in your own garden can be turned into a stunning focal point by planting a shade-tolerant wildflower meadow underneath. Ox-eye daisies, knapweed and musk mallow will all thrive in the dappled light and long grass. Drape a rustic rope-swing from a low-hanging limb and you will have another perfect shady vantage point from which to view your garden.

All-foliage plantings can lack a point of focus and appear rather bland until you get close up. You can transform the display from a distance by adding something to catch the eye. This could be anything from a gnarled old log in a naturalistic planting scheme, to a decorative, beehive-shaped compost bin in a country-style setting, or an elegant stone planter or statue in a contemporary garden.

To be most effective, make sure the feature is in keeping and in proportion with its surroundings. One trick is to have only part of the feature on view, so that it draws the onlooker in – maybe standing it on a hidden plinth or other raised platform to maximize the impact.

Arches are useful too. You can use them as a mock gateway between borders to separate different parts of the garden, or place them part-way down the vista to frame a statue or ornamental urn. Reinforce the effect by covering the arch with a climber with a neat outline and simple flower colour, so that it is not too distracting. At a boundary edge, an arch can be positioned

can create a convincing shady-glade or country-meadow feel.

Overhanging trees from the street or a neighbour's garden can be put to good use, too. Here, create a shady retreat under the dappled canopy using woodland-edge plants, such as foxgloves and shade-tolerant perennials.

Here, the colour of the chair has been carefully chosen to make an impact on the greens and to echo the red of the ornamental rhubarb.

Make the most of garden features to add depth and the illusion of space in a planting scheme, transforming potentially dingy corners into areas of charm and interest.

Landscaping materials such as pebbles, gravel and paving are other ways to introduce extra light into a dark corner. Pale-coloured paving can be used to attract attention to a particular feature or focal point, or to emphasize darker-leaved plants nearby.

For example, you could create a secluded sanctuary with an oriental feel using pale-stemmed bamboos, bright Japanese acers and stepping stones leading through a white sea of raked stone chippings to a pale grey lantern set on a rocky plinth.

On the other hand, cool, sun-bleached pebbles associate particularly well with the still waters of a mirrored pond (*see* box, page 27), especially when surrounded by lush ground-cover plants, like hostas.

so that it appears to access another part of the garden, creating the illusion that the garden is bigger than it really is.

Illuminating dark corners

Nearly every garden has at least one dark corner where plants remain inconspicuous in the gloom. You could make a feature of the low light levels by planting a brilliant white, multi-stemmed tree, such as silver birch, that will glow iridescently. Lighter features draw the eye, so a pale stone statue on a plinth, surrounded by the glossy, light-reflecting dark-green foliage of fatsia can look impressive.

A ferny grotto

An area of permanent shade can be transformed by creating a grotto using hardy ferns and other foliage shade-lovers. Dark, dank, ferny grottos should be cool and mysterious, preferably with the drumming of dripping water on stone and the smell of damp leaf mould underfoot. Casually scattered, half-rotten logs – complete with bracket fungi – add to the effect.

Use the differences in size of various ferns to create a dramatic sense of scale. For example, *Osmunda regalis* (royal fern) produces man-sized shuttlecocks, while the diminutive *Athyrium niponicum* var. *pictum* (Japanese painted fern) barely gets above your ankles. Then there's the

imposing tree fern dicksonia, which can be used to add stunning points of focus.

Emphasize the variations in the green palette by juxtaposing contrasts, such as the eerily dark-green *Polystichum aculeatum* (hard shield fern) against the lime-green shuttlecocks of *Matteuccia struthiopteris* (ostrich fern). Also mix leaf forms by setting ferns with paddle-shaped leaves, such as *Asplenium scolopendrium* (hart's tongue fern), next to ferns with finely cut foliage, like *Athyrium filix-femina* (lady fern).

Achieve subtle changes through the seasons by combining deciduous and evergreen varieties, as well as choosing ferns that change colour, such as *Dryopteris affinis* (golden male fern), which emerges gold and matures to dark green.

Planting schemes

Most successful garden designs have a strong connection with their surroundings. They echo the environment and setting, incorporating elements from structures and designs nearby. In a shady garden, it is important to introduce as much light as possible by choosing paler materials and light-reflecting plants, as well as features that will increase the sense of perspective.

Hydrangea anomala subsp. *petiolaris* – one of the most useful climbers in any shady setting.

Permanent shade border

North-facing borders running alongside walls and fences are in the permanent shadow of solid structures. They are also often long and straight, making them difficult to plant effectively. Between buildings you may also have to cope with buffeting air currents throughout the year as well as severe wind-chill in winter.

To make these borders more interesting, you need to break up the linear flow. In practice this means disguising the straight lines by planting the edges with evergreen foliage plants to soften and soothe, while planting something bolder elsewhere to distract the eye. Alongside paving, use the foliage spilling over the edge of the border to introduce curves into the design and add points of focus that are natural interruptions to the view.

Don't forget that the vertical structures are an opportunity to grow more plants. Use climbers that provide more than short periods of interest, and combine deciduous and evergreen varieties to achieve an ever-changing, yet continuous, display. In passageways, use pale-coloured foliage and plants with small leaves to increase the illusion of space.

PERMANENT SHADE BORDER (6M/20FT X 2M/6FT)

The climbing hydrangea is a shady star, providing year-round interest and the perfect backdrop to a permanently shaded border. To extend the season, it has been combined here with the versatile climbing rose 'Madame Alfred Carrière', which provides late-summer colour, and Boston ivy, for dramatic autumn foliage tints. In front, a combination of deciduous and evergreen shrubs and perennials add light, colour and interest throughout the year.

1 *Hydrangea anomala* subsp. *petiolaris*
2 *Rosa* 'Madame Alfred Carrière'
3 *Parthenocissus tricuspidata*
4 *Hosta sieboldiana* var. *elegans* (x 5)
5 *Euonymus fortunei* 'Emerald 'n' Gold'
6 *Athyrium niponicum* var. *pictum* (x 5)
7 *Skimmia* × *confusa* 'Kew Green' (x 3)
8 *Pulmonaria* 'Sissinghurst White' (x 3)
9 *Cornus alba* 'Elegantissima'
10 *Lamium maculatum* 'White Nancy' (x 5)

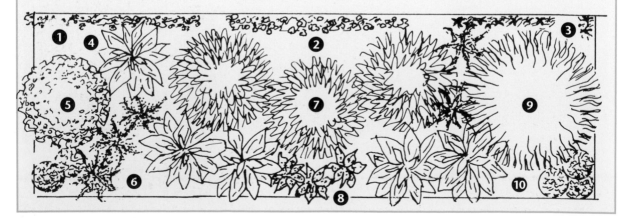

Dappled shade

To create a natural-looking woodland garden offering dappled shade takes as much thought and planning as any other garden design. If your garden is large enough, you can plant a mini copse of trees like the one featured here. Use small trees with open canopies such as birch, crab apples, hawthorn or mountain ash and plant them close. Where space is limited, you could buy a single multi-stemmed tree to create the woodland atmosphere, or train one yourself from a single-stemmed specimen.

On a smaller scale, you can create a woodland effect around tall-growing shrubs, such as amelanchier, witch

hazel, mock orange or viburnum. You may need to carry out some judicious pruning from time to time to open up the canopy, removing whole stems to the base rather than giving them a short-back-and-sides. Try to

Betula utilis var. *jacquemontii* – beautiful with and without its leaves.

mimic the tiered effect you find at a woodland edge when choosing the other plants to include in the scheme.

DAPPLED SHADE – CIRCULAR BED (6M/18FT ACROSS)

Based around a trio of lovely, elegant birch trees with striking brilliant white bark, this dappled bed provides an ever-changing display from early spring until late autumn with pink, purple and white flowers predominating. It could form the central feature in a large lawn, be incorporated towards one side of a smaller garden where it might merge with a shady boundary, or provide a cool oasis in the corner of a sunny plot.

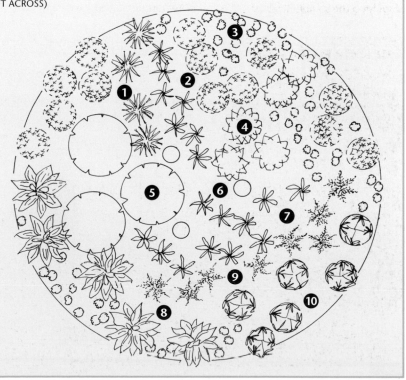

1 *Leucojum aestivum* (x 4)
2 *Campanula carpatica* f. *alba* 'Weisse Clips' (x 13)
3 *Anemone nemorosa* (x 50)
4 *Anemone* × *hybrida* 'Königin Charlotte' (x 3)
5 *Paeonia lactiflora* 'Bowl of Beauty' (x 3)
6 *Betula utilis* var. *jacquemontii* (x 3)
7 *Digitalis purpurea* Giant Spotted Group (x 18)
8 *Hosta* 'Francee' (x 5)
9 *Dryopteris erythrosora* (x 8)
10 *Helleborus niger* (x 6)

Dry, shady corner bed

Perhaps the most challenging areas of the garden are those in deep shade where the soil is dry. Under overhanging trees, especially evergreens, and areas at the foot of tall hedges and alongside north-facing walls are typical examples. However, if you look more carefully such places are often more sheltered and protected than the rest of the garden; if you take steps to alleviate the drawbacks you can make the most of the opportunities they offer.

The key to success, here, is to improve the moisture-holding capacity of the soil by digging in plenty of well-rotted organic matter before planting and mulching generously afterwards. Creating planting pockets in otherwise root-riddled soil may be necessary in some situations, while installing a watering system may also be worth considering.

Sarcococca confusa – a stalwart of dry, shady areas – is grown for its fragrance, winter flowers and spherical fruits.

Where possible, open up the area by pruning back overhanging canopies to let in more light. If the shadow is cast by your own buildings and other structures, brighten up the area by using a pale shade of stain or masonry paint, or perhaps by incorporating light-reflecting mirrors into your design.

Turn the surroundings into a pleasing backdrop rather than an eyesore.

Most important of all, it is essential to select plants that can cope with the demanding situation.

DRY, SHADY CORNER BED (5M/16FT X 3M/10FT)

A combination of variegated and glossy-leaved evergreen foliage plants helps brighten the darkness and create the illusion of air and light in this confined, dry and shady spot. The sense of space is reinforced by the dramatic use of contrasting leaf size and foliage texture. Seasonal highlights from spring, summer, autumn and winter flowers ring the changes through the year.

1 *Fatsia japonica*
2 *Hedera colchica* 'Dentata Variegata'
3 *Parthenocissus henryana*
4 *Digitalis purpurea* f. *albiflora* (x 6)
5 *Sarcococca confusa*
6 *Euonymus fortunei* 'Emerald Gaiety' (x 3)
7 *Geranium phaeum* 'Album' (x 6)
8 *Epimedium* × *youngianum* 'Niveum' (x 6)
9 *Convallaria majalis* (x 6)

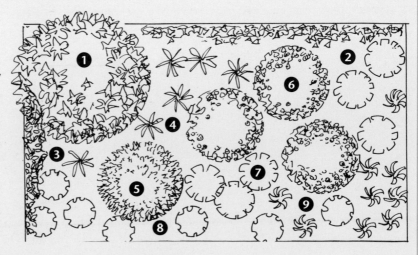

Shady courtyard

Many town and city courtyard gardens suffer from long periods of continuous shade from the surrounding buildings. Elsewhere, high boundary walls and outbuildings may create similar challenges for the gardener.

Soil can be exhausted and lacking in nutrients from many years of neglect or over-cultivation. It can be dry, too, not because the soil is particularly free draining, but because the buildings may prevent driving rain from reaching the ground, with any run-off diverted into the drainage system before it has had a chance to soak down into the soil.

On the bright side, city gardens enjoy a milder climate than those in the country, so you can grow a wider range of plants. Pest and disease problems may be reduced too, because the plants are more isolated.

Simple geometric shapes and restricted space means that courtyard gardens lend themselves to formal designs, which help distract the eye and create the illusion of space.

Consider introducing water features (see page 36) to make the most of reflected light, while creating a calming atmosphere, and perhaps using running water to drown out the background drone of traffic – often a drawback of urban gardens.

The neatness and formality of clipped box works well in nearly all courtyard settings.

SHADY COURTYARD (7M/21FT X 5.5M/17FT)

This simple, formal courtyard has been designed to make the most of available space while providing year-round interest with the greatest variety of plants possible. The climbers help disguise and break up the dominating impact of the surrounding walls, while specimen shrubs in containers offer a point of focus at different times of the year.

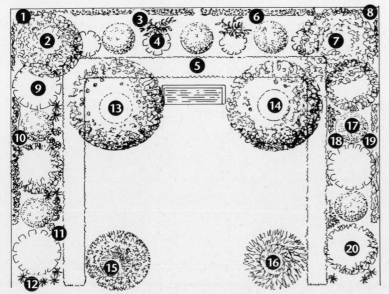

1 *Clematis* 'Willy'
2 *Daphne bholua* 'Jacqueline Postill'
3 *Chaenomeles speciosa* 'Nivalis' (x 2)
4 *Geranium macrorrhizum* 'Album' (x 4)
5 *Buxus sempervirens* (trimmed formal hedge)
6 *Polygonatum* × *hybridum* (x 2)
7 *Camellia* × *williamsii* 'Debbie'
8 *Clematis* 'Frances Rivis'
9 *Geranium psilostemon* (x 3)
10 *Rosa* 'Madame Grégoire Staechelin'
11 *Cyclamen hederifolium* (x 10) underplanted with *Tulipa* 'White Triumphator' (x 25)
12 *Liriope muscari* (x 10)
13 *Magnolia stellata* (in container)
14 *Hydrangea macrophylla* 'Mariesii Perfecta' (in container)
15 *Skimmia japonica* 'Rubella' (in container)
16 *Sarcococca confusa* (in container)
17 *Buxus sempervirens* (formal box topiary) (x 7)
18 *Vinca minor* (x 4) underplanted with *Tulipa* 'White Triumphator' (x 25)
19 *Clematis* 'Lasurstern'
20 *Campanula lactiflora* 'Prichard's Variety' (x 3)

Water in shade

Adding a water feature or pond to a shady area really gives it a lift. Not only does the water's surface help reflect the available light, but it will transform the atmosphere too.

Ponds

You will have to pick your spot carefully in a shady garden. Most pond plants require good light to thrive and the falling autumn leaves of deciduous trees play havoc with the quality of the water. Remember that evergreens, too, shed some of their leaves in early summer – holly, laurel and rhododendron, for example. Ideally, position your pond where it will get direct sunlight for at least one-third of the day.

Streams and waterfalls

Streams work particularly well in shade, especially if there are natural contours to follow. If possible, create a gently meandering gully running down a slight slope. At the bottom, install a submersible pump in a hidden reservoir to pump a steady flow of water for the stream. The reservoir needs to be large enough to hold all the water in the stream, otherwise it will flood when the pump is turned off. You will need a smaller hidden reservoir at the top to form the source of the stream. Place rocks and pebbles in the stream to slow the flow of water and create a whispering background gurgle.

On steeper slopes use a series of waterfalls and small pools to negotiate the drop. Make sure the lip of each fall is perfectly level so that the water flows evenly over it. Lay narrow strips of butyl rubber pond liner on top of underlay in the prepared gully, starting at the bottom and overlapping the pieces along the length of the stream and behind the vertical surface of waterfalls so that the watercourse is watertight.

HOW TO build a pond

You can use rigid, preformed liners or a flexible sheet liner. The advantage of a flexible liner is that it can be used to create any shape of pond you like, but the downside is that it requires more skill to get it right.

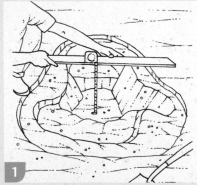

1 Excavate the soil for the whole area of the pond to 23cm (9in) – the depth of the shelves to hold marginal aquatic plants. Check levels with a spirit-level. Mark the deeper, central area of the pond and excavate this to 50–60cm (20–24in). Angle the vertical sides between the different levels so that they slope slightly towards the centre of the pond.

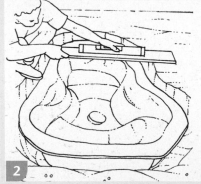

2 Remove any stones or other debris before lining the hole with builders' sand, loft insulation or a special pond-liner underlay. Test the fitting of the pond liner and check it with the spirit-level.

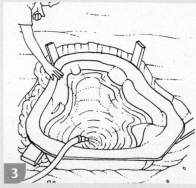

3 When you are ready to install the liner, place it in the hole. Backfill with earth and, ideally, with sand. Watering the sand in situ will help to ensure that it compacts under the liner. Slowly fill the liner with water from a hose.

Planting by shady water

How you plant the areas around shady water features is critical to their success. Try to combine shade-loving flowering perennials, such as primulas, sweet rocket, erythroniums and foxgloves, with those that offer more permanent foliage cover to achieve a feature that looks good all year.

Sweet flag, particularly the variegated form *Acorus calamus* 'Argenteostriatus', will illuminate the margin of a pond, or for a larger feature the more invasive umbrella grass is worth considering. Water irises such as 'Snowdrift' will bloom in partial shade too. *Calla palustris* is particularly useful for hiding the edges of a shady pond, although flowering may be reduced in the low light conditions.

Lush foliage plants such as hostas and rodgersias will accentuate the cool atmosphere, while the bright-yellow flowering spathes of *Lysichiton*

Make the most of lush plantings around ponds and other water features to help integrate them into the garden.

americanus (skunk cabbage) can be used to create seasonal talking points.

Hardy ferns in particular look great next to water. For example, *Osmunda regalis* (royal fern) would be an excellent choice to plant alongside a natural water feature where the soil remains damp, or consider the vigorous *Matteuccia struthiopteris* (ostrich fern) for larger areas.

The soil around artificial ponds and streams made with a waterproof liner

tends to remain drier than the surrounding areas, so here choose species such as *Dryopteris filix-mas* (male fern), *Polystichum aculeatum* (hard shield fern) and *Dryopteris erythrosora* (buckler fern).

Growing bog plants in dry shade

Transform a dry shady area by installing a bog garden. This is basically a permanently moist area of soil, created by excavating a hole and lining it with a butyl rubber pond liner on top of underlay.

Make several holes at the deepest point to allow for excess water to drain out or put a 5cm (2in) deep layer of pea shingle in the bottom. Then fill with a 3:1 mixture of good garden soil and well-rotted organic matter, augmented with a balanced fertilizer such as blood, fish and bone.

Starting at the middle, plant with shade-tolerant bog plants such as astilbes, hostas, primulas, lady's smock (cardamine), ligularias, *Lobelia* 'Queen Victoria', and mulch well after planting. Protect vulnerable plants from slugs, if these are a pest in your garden.

It is important to keep a bog garden evenly watered. This is easiest to achieve by laying a seep-hose just below the surface mulch, then either attach a hosepipe to apply water or plumb it into an automatic watering system.

Making a rill

In a formal shady garden, narrow strips of water between paving can look very effective and they are easy to create before laying the paving.

Dig out the gully and line it with a narrow strip of black butyl rubber pond liner on top of underlay so there are no creases. Make sure the edges are hidden by the paving which is laid along the edges, overlapping the gully by a few centimetres. Fill with water.

if you want moving water in the rill, the bottom of the gully will need a slight gradient to a reservoir containing a submersible pump.

For a really spectacular effect, add underwater lights.

Planting and growing

Once you have grappled with the various types of shade and understood how they offer different opportunities and challenges, you need to consider the fundamentals and practicalities of growing plants in the shadowlands. How, what, where and when are all key questions, as well as who's going to do the work, of course. You have to go back to the basics of what type of soil you have and how much moisture it holds. How can it be improved for the plants you want to grow? Where is the best place to plant and when? Also consider what problems your new charges are likely to encounter and how to get them off to the best possible start.

Garden soil

A successful shady garden is like any other garden; it depends to a large extent on its soil. Although this is largely dictated by the underlying soil profile, other factors come into play too. Under beech trees, for example, the decaying leaf litter tends to make the soil more acidic. Most deciduous trees are not so problematic, and the soils beneath them tend to contain more organic matter than soils in the open. However, they are invariably drier and more impoverished because the tree roots take moisture and nutrients from them, and the overhanging canopy protects the area from rain.

Acid or alkaline?

Before making plant selections, it is essential that you know how acidic or alkaline (limy) your soil is, as some plants are lime-haters (rhododendrons, for example), and some (such as lilacs) are lime-lovers. This is measured by the pH scale, which ranges from 0 to 14. The mid-point of 7 is neutral; readings above 7 indicate increasing alkalinity, readings below 7 indicate increasing acidity. Fortunately, most plants will grow happily in soils with a pH of between 5.5 (slightly acidic) and 7.5 (slightly alkaline).

To test your garden soil, collect about five samples from different parts of the border, being sure to dig down about 15cm (6in) to avoid contamination by recent fertilizer

Use a soil-test kit, available in any garden centre, to check the pH level of the soil in your garden before you decide which plants to buy.

Checking garden soil

Try these two ready-reckoner tests to check what type of soil you have in your garden and how well it drains.

DRAINAGE
Dig a series of 30cm (12in) deep holes across the area and fill with water. Leave 24 hours.

If the hole is empty your soil drains freely; if there is water in the bottom you may have a drainage problem and should consider ways to solve it – such as digging deeply and incorporating horticultural grit or installing land drains

SOIL TYPE
Wet a small amount of soil and rub it between finger and thumb.

If it feels gritty, it contains sand; if it feels silky, it contains a lot of silt; and if it feels smooth or sticky there are plenty of clay particles in it

Soil types

HEAVY SOILS
- Comprise a high proportion of clay particles that are packed tightly together
- Few air spaces
- Poor drainage
- Fertile
- Difficult to work, especially after rain, when they become sticky
- Easily compacted when walked on

LIGHT SOILS
- Comprise mainly larger, irregularly shaped sandy particles
- Lots of air spaces
- Good drainage
- Water-soluble nutrients are easily washed out (a process known as leaching), so can become impoverished
- Easy to cultivate, even during the winter, and warm up quickly, so are ideal for early sowings outdoors in spring

SILTY SOILS
- Comprise particles falling between sand and clay in size and shape
- Usually fertile
- Good drainage
- Do not dry out quickly
- Easily compacted when walked on

LOAMY SOILS
- Ideal balance of different size particles, up to 25 per cent clay particles
- Very fertile
- Good drainage
- Do not dry out quickly
- Not easily compacted

PEATY SOILS
- Acid
- Rich in organic matter
- Dark colour, so warm quickly in spring
- Moist or wet
- Not easily compacted

CHALKY SOILS
- Alkaline
- Moderately fertile
- Very free-draining
- Often shallow over bedrock of chalk
- Low in organic matter

applications, decaying leaf litter or mulch. Next sieve and mix the samples before testing to get an average sample of the area. If you are testing a whole garden, make sure you do the areas with different levels of shade separately. You may find variations between these areas as well as across the garden.

Reducing/increasing acidity

In most circumstances, you can reduce the acidity of soil by adding lime. However, you cannot do this under trees where the surface soil is full of roots. Your only option, here, is to use spent mushroom compost as alkaline soil conditioner and mulch. Where you are able to use lime, don't try making drastic changes all in one go, and make sure any applications occur several weeks before planting and that the lime is incorporated thoroughly. Don't apply lime at the same time as organic matter or

Buy the best spade you can afford (preferably stainless steel) as it makes digging much, much easier.

fertilizers, since they will react unfavourably with each other.

If you have an alkaline, chalky soil and want to make it more acid, you could dig in acidic organic materials such as composted pine-needles – but you will need a lot. Another option is to dig in sulphur chips and feed lime-hating plants each spring with chelated iron, but you will have to repeat the process annually to maintain the effect. All in all, it really is best to *improve* what you have rather than try to *change* it.

Improving soil

Nearly all soils in shade can be improved by adding well-rotted farmyard manure, garden compost, leafmould or spent mushroom compost. This stuff is the cure-all for most soil ills. It will increase the water-holding capacity and available nutrients in dry and impoverished soil in shade, as well as light, sandy soil elsewhere. It also improves the structure and drainage of heavy soils. In addition, organic matter increases the activity and populations of earthworms and other beneficial soil-borne creatures.

Handling manure may sound unappealing to the uninitiated, but when it is well rotted it is odourless and crumbly. If it stinks, it's not

Adding plenty of sharp sand or horticultural grit to heavy soils will help improve drainage and aeration.

ready to put on the soil. In fact, adding partly rotted organic matter to your soil will actually rob it of nitrogen because the micro-organisms consume this as they complete the breakdown of the organic matter in the soil. The traditional way of incorporating organic matter into soil used to be by digging it in, but more recent research suggests that for most soils the best option is to lay it on the surface and let the soil organisms do the work for you. This is the best option if the shady soil is full of roots from nearby shrubs and trees.

Very shallow soil can be improved by importing good-quality topsoil into the garden. However, in shady borders alongside the house you need to take care not to bridge the damp-course, and raising the soil level over the roots of established trees elsewhere in the garden can be detrimental, especially if the soil is piled against the trunk.

After planting, always mulch a shady border with a 5–7cm (2–3in)

the soil is cultivated to two blade depths (double digging). If lashings of well-rotted organic matter and horticultural grit are added to the bottom layer, this can be a good way of improving the drainage of heavy soils in shade. Digging can be made a lot quicker, but not necessarily more effective, by hiring a rotavator.

Digging in autumn exposes more of the soil to the weathering effects of winter frosts, which break up large clods of earth into workable soil by the spring. Lighter soils are better cultivated in spring, because this avoids loss of nutrients due to leaching over the winter months.

Recycling garden waste

Recycling garden waste makes good gardening sense as it's the best way of returning organic matter and nutrients to the soil, and saves money on soil improvers and mulches. If your garden is shaded by deciduous trees you will have an annual bounty of autumn leaves that can be gathered up and turned into really useful soil improver. All other organic waste, including most weeds, small pruning offcuts and grass clippings, can be recycled though a garden compost heap. Pernicious weeds

layer of well-rotted organic matter to help prevent moisture loss. This is particularly important when planting in dry shady areas under trees and alongside walls. Make sure new plants do not run short of moisture by watering regularly – giving the soil a good soaking – until they are well established. This may take a whole year in the most demanding shady sites under trees.

Soil cultivation

There are several methods of working soil. Which you choose will depend on your soil type, what you are trying to achieve and how much work you are prepared to do.

The lightest and easiest method is forking over the soil. This is less strenuous than digging with a spade, and the most effective way of cultivating shady soil that's full of roots from overhanging trees and nearby shrubs, as well as soil that's full of stones. It's also a useful way of cultivating lightly between perennials.

If there are no roots in the way, digging with a spade is more efficient. This can be either a matter of turning over the soil to a single blade depth (single digging), or creating a 30cm (12in) wide trench and forking over the bottom so that

Cover the waste in a compost bin with a piece of old carpet or tarpaulin to help protect it from heavy rains and speed the composting process.

with seedheads or roots should be burnt or placed in the garden-waste bin for collection.

Making garden compost

Turning garden waste into compost requires air, heat and water, along with beneficial bacteria contained in the waste. An efficient composting system facilitates a good balance of these. Organic matter will eventually rot down if it is simply piled up in a loose heap, but you will get quicker and more consistent results with a compost bin. It will also be neater and easier to manage.

Whether you buy a plastic or timber self-assembly bin (or make your own), it should hold at least 1cu. m (35cu. ft) of waste. At this size, the bin will heat up quickly,

Construct a leaf-mould bin out of thick plastic netting or galvanized chicken wire held in place by stout posts driven into the ground, and keep it covered.

making decomposition more efficient, and be large enough to hold the waste from an average-sized, shady garden.

If your garden is small or doesn't produce much organic waste, consider clubbing together with a neighbour rather than making do with a smaller bin. In larger gardens it is worth having two bins – one in the process of rotting and one in use.

Bear in mind that some proprietary plastic bins with tight-fitting lids do not allow sufficient air circulation or access for rainwater, so you may need to drill a few holes in it.

You can make your own compost bin out of lengths of second-hand timber that has been pressure-treated with wood preservative.

Making leaf mould

Either fill perforated black polythene bags and stash them out of sight behind the garden shed, or, if you have a lot of leaves to deal with, build a leaf-mould enclosure. Again, add soil to the bags or enclosure to speed up decomposition. Keep the leaves damp and in a year they should have rotted down and be ready to use in the garden.

Clear lawns of fallen leaves promptly to prevent the beleaguered grasses of a shady garden being smothered.

Composting tips

■ Stand the bin on bare soil so that soil-borne creatures can move in and out with ease.

■ You can fill the bin with almost any type of garden waste and most kitchen waste, but do not add cooked foods (other than vegetables), meat or fish, as these may attract vermin.

■ Avoid adding diseased plant material, perennial weed roots and weeds setting seed because these may survive the composting process and create more weed or disease problems in future years.

■ Woody prunings can be added, provided they are chopped finely using a pair of secateurs or a garden shredder. This will ensure they rot down at the same rate as the other material.

■ It is important that the compost does not get too wet in winter (cover an open-topped bin) or too dry in summer (add water if necessary).

■ Speed up the composting process by sprinkling on a proprietary compost activator, or adding a couple of spadefuls of rotted compost from the previous bin or good garden soil. This will introduce the micro-organisms necessary for quick composting.

■ Try to mix dry materials, such as prunings, and moist waste, such as lawn clippings, to prevent the heap getting overly wet or too dry. Or add them in alternate layers (each no more than 15cm/6in deep).

■ Winter cold will slow the composting process significantly, so it is worth insulating your compost bin with bubble polythene or old carpet.

■ Serious composters swear by turning the heap inside out after a month to ensure even composting, but for me life's too short!

Choosing plants for shade

When choosing a new plant for a particular position it is important to take into account the soil, aspect and space available – also, of course, whether it will be in full, partial or temporary shade. A plant in the wrong place will struggle to establish and if too big for the position will need constant cutting back. Prepare the soil before planting (*see* page 41) so that you can plant quickly and efficiently.

Bedding plants

Tender bedding is an essential pick-me-up for many a garden display in the summer months. Most need a sunny spot, but begonias and impatiens are good choices for shade, while for partially shaded areas you could try ageratum, antirrhinum, calendula, lobelia, pansies and stocks (*see also* pages 113–14). Look for stocky plants that are just showing flower buds.

Dozens of colourful varieties are available each spring as seedlings and tiny plants (or plugs), or as young plants sold in strips, trays and individual pots. Many annual

Make sure all bedding plants are acclimatized to the rigours of outdoor life by hardening them off gradually in a cold frame.

flowers are easy to raise from seed (*see* page 64), which is a cost-effective way of raising a lot of plants of one or two varieties.

Perennials

Perennials form a large and varied group and many species are well adapted to shady situations. Most are herbaceous and die back to ground level during the winter, but

some, such as ajugas, bergenias, epimediums, hellebores, lamiums and pulmonarias, keep their leaves

Don't forget

Hardy perennials, shrubs, climbers and trees can be planted at any time, provided the soil is not frozen or waterlogged. However, on well-drained soils planting in autumn is preferable because the plants have a chance to get established before the summer. On heavy clay, plant in spring once the soil becomes workable. On all soil types, conifers are best planted in mid- to late spring so that they have time to get established before the winter weather sets in.

Buying healthy plants

Avoid any of the following:
- Leggy, wilting or waterlogged plants
- Plants in full flower
- Plants with faded labels
- Pots with weeds growing in the top
- Plants with yellowing leaves, or any other signs of pest or disease attack
- Pots with lots of roots growing out of the bottom

Plant out shade-tolerant bedding into well-prepared soil that has been cleared of all weeds, including the roots. Take precautions against slugs if necessary.

during the winter months; some even flower. Perennials can be bought throughout the year, but the best time to get them is during early spring, when the new growth is apparent and the plants are small enough to handle safely.

Most perennials grow quickly so if you want just a few of each variety buy them as small, vigorous plants. For a more extensive display, save money by buying one or two much larger specimens and dividing them before planting. If you do buy herbaceous perennials in late winter before any growth is apparent, ensure you get new stock rather than left-over plants from last season. Many perennials are also available as seed, but although easy to raise they may take two years to flower.

Climbers

Some shade-tolerant climbers, such as ivies, ornamental vines and climbing hydrangeas, can tolerate deep shade, so are ideal for adding height and

Mulch the soil after planting with a thick layer of well-rotted organic matter, taking care not to pile it up against the stems as this may cause them to rot.

Wall shrubs, such as this flowering quince, should be carefully tied into the bottom of their support after planting, using soft garden string.

interest in the most demanding spots. Other popular climbers, including some clematis and climbing roses, are ideal for partially shaded areas of the garden. They can also be used to cover the ground between trees and shrubs.

Sun-loving climbers scrambling over pergolas and arches are useful for providing shady sanctuaries in sun-drenched gardens, too (*see* page 21). A wide range of climbers sold in containers can be planted at any time of the year, but always check that the plant has several strong-looking, undamaged stems.

Shrubs

Most successful shady-garden displays include a range of deciduous and evergreen shrubs that flower, fruit and offer foliage and bark interest at different times throughout the year. Many types of shrubs can tolerate partially shaded situations and a few will survive deep shade, including aucuba, box, mahonia, pachysandra, ruscus, sarcococca and symphoricarpos.

These days most shrubs are sold container-grown, but a few, notably conifers, can be bought rootballed – grown in a field and lifted with soil around a ball of roots. Some hedging

shrubs are also sold root-wrapped or bare-rooted in the autumn or early spring for immediate planting. Whatever shrub you buy, look for a well-balanced shape with healthy-looking foliage, and no signs of pest or disease.

Some shrubs, such as roses, are grafted and the union should be checked to make sure it is well healed and strong.

Trees

A tree can be an ideal way of providing long-term shade to a sunny garden. However, it takes up a lot of space and can dominate the

Don't forget

It is easy to be seduced by climbers and shrubs when in full bloom, so make sure they will earn their keep at other times.

overall design of the garden, so choose with care. Ideally, the tree chosen for a shady garden should look good all year round, such as snake-bark maples, silver birch and crab apples (*see* pages 115–18 for more suggestions).

Trees are sold in a variety of sizes: single-stem 'whips' with no side shoots from the main stem; slightly older young trees showing their first side branches (known as a feathered maiden); half-standards with a head of branches and a clear stem to about 1.2m (4ft); and a full standard with a more mature head of branches and a clear stem to 1.8m (6ft). Older 'heavy standards' and 'extra-heavy standards' are also available from some specialists. If you are laying out a garden from scratch, including a mature specimen tree in your plans can give an instant sense of permanence and structure to the overall display.

Don't forget

Larger trees are not only considerably more expensive to buy than smaller ones, but they will not establish as quickly and a small specimen may well overtake a much larger one after a few seasons.

Planting guides

BEDDING

Two weeks before planting out, harden off all young bedding plants that have been raised under cover. When they are acclimatized to outside conditions, water them thoroughly and allow to drain.

Remove the plant from its pot by holding it upside down, while supporting the rootball, and gently tap the side of the pot. If necessary, cut through the pot to remove it rather than damaging the delicate roots. Always handle the plant by holding the rootball rather than the stem or leaves.

Plant in the soil, ensuring that the crown is set at the same depth as it was in the pot, and lightly firm the soil with your fingers. Cover with horticultural fleece overnight if nights are cool and protect vulnerable plants from slugs (*see* page 63).

PERENNIALS

Water plants thoroughly before planting.

Perennials need room to spread, so make sure you space them sufficiently. This may mean the display looking a bit sparse in its first year but this can be overcome by sowing colourful annuals in between to provide cover.

Most perennials are shallow rooted (so you don't need to dig too deeply), but make sure the hole is wide – particularly when you are planting among other, established plants.

Set the crown of the plant at the same depth as it is in the pot and firm the soil well with your fingers.

After watering thoroughly, mulch the bare soil immediately around the crown without piling it against the stems.

Protect vulnerable plants from slugs.

CLIMBERS

Water thoroughly before planting.

Climbers to be trained up walls and fences will need to be planted about 45cm (18in) away from the support and set at an angle back towards it – train the climber up a short cane attached to the bottom of the main support. This will mean the rootball can expand into fresh soil on all sides and establish quickly.

With most climbers, set the crown at the same depth as the plant is in the pot. The exception to this rule is clematis, which should be planted 10–15cm (4–6in) deeper than they are in the pot to help protect against clematis wilt disease. Deeper planting also keeps the roots cool and moist, which clematis love.

After watering thoroughly, apply a thick mulch around each plant without piling it against the stems.

Climbers planted among established shrubs and trees should be planted in a large planting hole, cleared of roots, that has been lined with untreated, second-hand timber. This will give the climber time to get well established before the timber rots, allowing the roots of adjacent plants access.

SHRUBS AND TREES

Water thoroughly before knocking the rootball out of its pot.

Dig a hole that is about twice as wide and deep as the rootball.

Check that the top of the rootball is at the same height as the surrounding soil by laying a cane across the hole. Plant grafted roses deeper so that the graft is below soil level.

Backfill with soil and firm with your heel to remove any air pockets.

Water container plants before planting and make sure the hole is deep enough to keep the rootball at the same depth as it was in the pot.

After watering thoroughly, apply a thick mulch to cover a 45cm (18in) diameter circle around each plant without piling it against the stems. In exposed positions, put up a windbreak to protect the new shrub until well established.

For all trees over 1.5m (5ft) tall, hammer a short stake into the ground on the windward side of the main stem so that about 60cm (2ft) remains above the ground.

Use a special tree-tie with cushioned spacer to attach the tree trunk to the stake.

With a large rootball, angle the stake towards the trunk to avoid damaging it.

In a garden plagued by rabbits, slip a spiral tree guard around the trunk after planting to stop them stripping the bark and killing the tree.

To avoid damaging the rootball of trees, angle the supporting stake towards the trunk and secure with a specially cushioned tree-tie.

Growing fruit and vegetables in shade

Most fruit and vegetables need an open, sunny site to crop well. However, several types will grow in a shady garden or in the shadow areas of a sunny plot, although yields may be reduced. In permanently shaded areas, even if it's fairly bright, you will be limited to rhubarb, or herbs such as bay, mint and parsley.

If the shade lasts for no more than half the day you should be able to grow fruit crops such as blackberries, Morello cherries, gooseberries and raspberries. Vegetables that will produce a reasonable harvest in these conditions include beetroot, calabrese and kale. Salad crops such as lettuce and radish, plus thyme, rosemary and sage, can be grown too.

In areas of bright shade with some direct sun (east- and west-facing borders, for example), add cooking apples and strawberries to the menu, as well as marrows, courgettes and potatoes.

In areas of dappled light with some direct sun at either end of the day, you should be ble to grow all the crops already mentioned plus blackcurrants, redcurrants and whitecurrants, as well as sweet cherries and eating apples such as 'Discovery'.

Gooseberries can be grown in temporarily shaded areas of the garden, provided the bushes get direct sunlight for part of the day.

Light and colour play tricks on the eye in the shady garden. Take, for example, pale and pastel shades – in direct sunlight they can look flat, washed out and indistinguishable, but in shade they become rich in variation and hue.

Light levels affect each colour group in different ways.

Blues are best in shade, appearing cool and pure. In sun they can look purple or even mauve. Blues also seem to recede into the distance, helping create the sense of space in a shady garden.

Yellows, which appear simple and stark in direct sun, become uplifting and complex in shade – lemon yellows, with their touch of green, work particularly well at low light levels. All yellows appear much nearer to the eye than they really are, making them useful as a distraction, or for leading the eye.

Reds and **oranges** are hot and sultry in a sunny spot, creating a sense of drama, but become darker and more atmospheric in shade. In sun, red flowers dominate all around them, whereas in shade their impact is more subdued.

Pinks range from dilute red with a touch of yellow (warm peachy pinks) to watery red tinged with blue (cool shell pinks). In shade, pinks become cooler, so the peachy pinks tend to stand out and the shell pinks recede.

White, by contrast, is straightforward: bleached and indistinct in direct sun, it becomes the centre of attention in shade, adding glittering highlights with hidden depths and intricacies.

Purple, on the other hand, may be strong and purposeful in direct sun, but darkens to near-black invisibility in the shade.

Greens are the most important garden colours in sun or shade – the underrated backdrop or canvas on which all other colours are painted. They associate particularly well with yellows and blues, and tone down reds and purples.

Verdant shades are the perfect backdrop to all other colours.
① **Harmonize** with the cool blue and yellow of polyanthus in spring.
② **Contrast** with the rich rusty reds of autumnal sedums.
③ **Reinforce** with warm purple alliums during early summer.

Changing light levels

Light changes continuously. The prevailing weather conditions play their part, of course, but light also varies through the day. At dusk and dawn, when sunlight passes obliquely though the atmosphere, light is warm in colour and soft. Shaded areas are darker at these times. In the middle of the day, when the sun is overhead, colours appear colder and harder.

As the seasons change, so does the light. During the spring the light is cooler and clearer, which makes the pure colours of spring bulbs stand out. By summer the light is harsh and fierce, except at either end of the day when it is warm and inviting. During the autumn light softens and becomes diffused, whereas in winter it is full of stark contrasts – or becomes dim and watery.

Containers

Containers are a great way of adding colour, height and interest to shady areas. They also enable you to grow plants that might otherwise struggle in your garden, and provide an opportunity for constantly changing displays. Indeed, if you are gardening in a shady courtyard, or on a balcony, containers may well be your only option.

Match the plants carefully to the containers to make the most of the display. For example, for a simple pot with limited decoration, choose a showgirl of a plant such as a flamboyant lily, which simply demands attention. Ornate pots, on the other hand, often look most effective when filled with elegant foliage plants with clean outlines, such as hostas.

Try to make the most of colourful pot glazes by choosing plants with flowers or foliage of a similar or complementary shade, and exploit textures by using contrasting foliage. By combining flowering, foliage, evergreen and deciduous plants you can create displays that will last throughout the year. Alternatively, for real impact, choose plants that flower at the same time or have a unifying element.

Trees

Imposing trees can have a dramatic impact on a garden's atmosphere and your enjoyment of it. When grown in pots they can be used as mobile parasols, providing dappled shade wherever you want it. These days, heavy-duty, lockable castors that can be fitted to sturdy wooden tubs are available, so you can move the tree around and secure it in position with ease. Otherwise, grow a tree in an ordinary container and use a pot mover to shift it around.

Choose trees with umbrella-shaped canopies such as certain crab apples or flowering cherries to provide maximum shade. Multi-stemmed trees such as *Betula pendula* (silver birch), eucalyptus or *Rhus typhina* (stag's horn sumach) not only look impressive in a container but will be more stable.

It is usually impractical to repot container trees, so, instead, remove the top 10cm (4in) of compost every few years and replace with fresh.

Shrubs

Mature shrubs provide a permanent framework to the shady patio display. Flowering shrubs can have real impact on shady parts of the garden when in bloom and are useful as a foil for other plants at other times. Sun-loving flowering shrubs can be raised in pots in a sunny spot then moved into a shaded area just as they are coming into flower.

Choose a container at least 45cm (18in) wide and deep for most shrubs. Once established, very little extra care needs to be given to them. If the shrub becomes pot-bound, repot

Choose a plant to complement the container: here the bold outlines of blue-leaved hostas are the perfect partners for stylish copper cones.

during spring either in the same sized or a slightly larger container. If this is impractical, replace the top 5cm (2in) of compost every few years.

Climbers

Container-grown climbers are useful for providing an instant focal point, breaking up ugly expanses of wall or giving temporary privacy. Many popular flowering climbers, such as clematis and summer jasmine, are ideal for light shade or areas of temporary shade that get at least some direct sunlight for part of the day. Annual climbers such as black-eyed Susan, sweet peas and climbing nasturtiums can also grow and flower well in dappled shade.

For areas of deeper shade there is a wide selection of variegated ivies – the small-leaved varieties can look enchanting trained over a special mesh support as a kind of mock topiary.

Shade-lovers planted in pots are another way of livening up a sunless border or woodland edge.

Climbers trained up vertical supports such as a wigwam of bamboo canes should be planted in a wide container. Less vigorous climbers, on the other hand, can be allowed to cascade from tall urns to good effect, or in the case of small-leaved ivy, used to soften the edges of hanging baskets and window-boxes in shady locations. As a rule, larger pots are easier to look after, although you can grow annual climbers in quite small pots – provided you can keep up with the watering.

Annuals and perennials

Annual bedding plants and perennial flowers, which provide much of the floral interest in sunny pots and containers, are more reluctant to put on a show in shade. The best annuals and biennials for lightly shaded areas include *Begonia semperflorens*, impatiens (busy lizzie), lobelia, mimulus (monkey flower), coleus, myosotis (forget-me-not), phlox, nicotiana (tobacco plant), polyanthus

and viola. Good flowering perennials for lightly shaded containers include lamium (dead nettle) and pulmonaria (lungwort). Aquilegia (columbine) and astrantia (masterwort) will cope in areas of deep shade.

Where you want foliage interest go for melianthus (honey bush), *Lysimachia nummularia* (creeping Jenny), glechoma (variegated ground ivy), hosta and houttuynia, and there are the ornamental brassicas for winter interest.

Bulbs

Nothing can match the impact of a container filled with bulbs in full bloom. Many bulbs are sun-worshippers, but there are a few gems that will thrive in a shady spot provided they get some direct sunlight for at least part of the day. The key to success with most bulbs is to keep the

displays simple and cram in as many bulbs as possible. Scillas, hyacinths, lilies, grape hyacinths and daffodils will all flower in permanent containers kept in temporary shade (up to half the day). Tulips will also perform well if they are moved into a sunny position after flowering (where they can rebuild their reserves for next year).

Although bulbs have a relatively short flowering season, you can create a succession of colour by planting several varieties with different flowering times in the same container. To squeeze as many bulbs in as possible, take advantage of the fact that different kinds need to be planted at different depths by planting them in layers. In more permanent shade, go for the really shade-tolerant bulbs, such as cyclamens and snowdrops, which are well adapted to life under the canopy.

Grasses and bamboos

Ornamental grasses make unusual, but effective, container plants with their elegant, cascading fountains of colourful foliage and dramatic late-summer flowers. Many grasses are sufficiently drought tolerant to cope with life in containers, but only a handful will thrive in the shade. One is *Carex* 'Evergold'. *Hakonechloa macra* 'Alboaurea' (hakone grass), with its tapering, yellow-variegated leaves, makes a pleasing specimen in a pot, with its shaggy mop of foliage.

Growing bamboos in pots allows you to include invasive species without risk of them getting out of hand. *Sasa palmata* (palm bamboo), for example, can be too vigorous in a small garden, but in a pot can be kept in check and will add a jungle atmosphere wherever its used – even in deep shade. Perhaps the best bamboo for a container is the less invasive *Fargesia murielae* (umbrella bamboo), which produces a miniature clump of yellowish, arching canes clothed in small leaves that have a pleasing, softening effect in a courtyard setting.

It is important not to overfeed grasses and bamboos in containers. Make sure they are sheltered from cold or drying winds, which can scorch the edges of the leaves. In winter, stand pots on 'pot-feet' to help excess moisture drain from the compost and prevent the crowns rotting.

Some grasses need to be cut right down in spring, but most require little more than a trim. They will look a whole lot neater though if you comb through the foliage to remove any dead stems, leaves and other debris. To keep established grasses vigorous, tip them out of the pot every few years and divide the clump.

Ferns

Dwarf hardy ferns can make excellent container plants for deep shade, providing a foil for other shade-tolerant plants. Ideal for transforming dark, north-facing corners, they come in a surprising range of shades, textures, shapes and sizes, and combine well with hostas and other shade-loving perennial and bedding plants, as well as spring bulbs such as anemones and daffodils.

Try one of the hart's tongue ferns such as *Asplenium scolopendrium* Cristatum Group for its paddle-shaped, bright-green fronds with distinctive wavy margins, or a shuttlecock fern, such as *Dryopteris affinis* or *Polystichum aculeatum*. A trunk-forming, palm-like fern such as *Blechnum chilense* in a feature tub is a good shady focal point.

Ferns can be grown in containers of almost any size, filled with peat-based multipurpose or loam-based John Innes compost. Once established they do not require much attention, but don't allow them to dry out. Avoid high-nitrogen fertilizers as this encourages soft growth that is prone to damage and disease.

General maintenance

Just because shade-loving plants seem as tough as old boots doesn't mean you can plant them and leave them to their own devices. It is crucial that you water even well-adapted plants in shady, dry soil regularly until really established – which can take many months in the most demanding situations. Thereafter, you can improve displays through judicious dead-heading, pruning and applying an annual mulch.

Mulching

This is one of the most important tasks in a shady garden. There are three types of mulch (a loose layer of material placed on the surface of the soil): organic, such as well-rotted garden compost or leaf mould; inorganic, such as gravel and pebbles; and sheet mulch, such as fabric or black polythene.

Mulching suppresses weeds, reduces moisture loss from the soil through evaporation, and acts as an insulator, keeping the soil warmer in winter and cooler in summer. You can apply mulch in autumn when the soil is warm and moist, or in spring, just as it is starting to warm up. Loose organic mulches will help improve the soil as it breaks down by feeding earthworms and other beneficial soil-borne creatures, as well as increasing the nutrients and water-holding capacity of the soil, counteracting the two main shortcomings of a dry, shady soil.

Sheet mulches are less easy on the eye, but useful nonetheless for covering the ground when planting up inaccessible shady areas at the bottom of the garden. If planting a new area, simply lay down the sheet over the area before planting through cross-shaped slits. You can disguise the sheet with a shallow layer of chipped bark.

Even woody plants, such as roses, can get tall and lanky in shade and will benefit from support with a stake when in flower, or during the winter to prevent windrock.

Staking

Perennials planted in shade tend to grow taller and lankier than they do in the sun, so they are more prone to flopping when in full flower, and their stems may become drawn and weak. Shade-loving perennials that may need staking include peonies and trollius.

Plants can be supported using either individual stakes (useful for varieties that produce tall flower spikes and top-heavy individual blooms) or clump supports. These are designed for multi-stemmed or clump-forming perennials, but can also be used for closely planted, individual-stemmed perennials such

Mulching is the key to success in any garden, shady or otherwise, as it not only feeds the soil and the plants, but prevents weeds and moisture loss in summer and insulates roots in winter. It is an ideal job for the winter months too.

Clump-forming perennials in shade that are prone to flopping when in full bloom can be supported during spring using special linking stakes

up the clump when it's in full bloom, with the support pushed 15cm (6in) into the ground. Position the support during the spring when the plant is starting to shoot and within a few weeks it will be hidden. All supports can be removed after flowering or in autumn. Note down where supports have been unsuccessful or too intrusive so you can make improvements the following year.

as lilies. Tie individual stakes (which should be long enough to go about 30cm (12in) into the ground) to the budding flower spike just below the head. Next, secure with soft string, tying it tightly around the support and loosely around the plant.

Clump-supports come in different sizes and need to match the plant both in size and strength. The support should reach about halfway

Don't forget

You can avoid the need for staking by selecting stocky, self-supporting perennials such as alchemilla (lady's mantle), begonia, brunnera, dicentra (bleeding heart), euphorbia, hardy geranium, hellebore, heuchera, hosta, Japanese anemone, liriope (lilyturf), phlox, polygonatum (Solonon's seal), pulmonaria (lungwort), sedum and veronica.

Dead-heading

Flowers are at a premium in shade, so it is worth doing everything you can to improve performance. Removing the fading flowers will not only make beds and borders look neater, but it will encourage the plants to flower for longer as they are not putting their energies into producing seed. This is particularly so with annuals such as sweet peas, which will stop flowering altogether if they are not dead-headed routinely. Although it is worth removing the unsightly dying flowers of some large-flowered plants, including pelargonium, dead-heading bedding plants in general simply isn't feasible.

Some shade-loving perennials *are* worth dead-heading. With those that produce flower spikes, such as foxgloves, cut the fading flower back if there is a younger side shoot lower down, which will bloom later.

Most bulbs are worth dead-heading if you have the patience, though a few, including alliums, have ornamental seedheads, which are worth retaining. If you do decide to dead-head, remove only the bloom itself and leave the green stem and leaves to photosynthesize for at least six weeks and build up the necessary reserves to flower well the following season.

A number of repeat-flowering shrubs and climbers, particularly

For a more natural look, use short pruning off-cuts and a cat's-cradle of soft string, or insert twiggy prunings around clumps just as new shoots emerge in spring.

Improve the appearance and future performance of repeat-flowering plants such as pelargonium by regular dead-heading.

roses, benefit from dead-heading to keep the display neat and help prolong flowering. Either break off the faded flowers or use secateurs to remove them. Those that produce attractive seedheads or colourful fruits (or hips) can be left.

Shrubs with lots of tiny flowers can be trimmed lightly with shears after flowering is over. Take care when dealing with rhododendrons and

Some shrubs, such as this cornus, produce better displays if kept young and vigorous by pruning right back to a stubby framework.

magnolias because they produce next year's flowers just below the fading blooms. With hydrangeas, delay dead-heading until after the worst of the winter weather as the old flower spikes look attractive in the winter garden and will help protect next year's flower buds.

Pruning

Many woody shrubs and climbers grown in the shade will require regular pruning to keep them in good shape and performing well.

How you go about pruning will depend on what particular attribute you are aiming to promote. A number of shade-tolerant shrubs, including *Aucuba japonica*, *Berberis thunbergii*, *Euonymus fortunei*, *Fatsia japonica*, *Magnolia stellata*, *Sarcococca confusa*, *Skimmia japonica* and *Viburnum plicatum* f. *tomentosum* 'Mariesii' don't need pruning at all and are a good choice for novice gardeners.

Pruning for flowers

Shrubs that flower early in the summer, philadelphus and escallonia, for example, do so on the previous season's stems. This means they have to be pruned directly after flowering. Cut back about one-third of the stems, starting with the oldest, to a younger sideshoot lower down or to a healthy-looking, outward-facing bud.

Pruning modern bush roses

These need pruning during early spring to keep them flowering well. First remove all dead, diseased and damaged stems, as well as any that are weak or cross the centre, then proceed as follows.

Large-flowered (hybrid tea) bush roses Cut all new growth back by about half.

Cluster-flowered (floribunda) bush roses Cut only the oldest stems hard back, with the remainder cut back to about 45cm (18in). Each time, cut back to about 0.5cm (¼in) above an outward-facing bud.

Well-established climbing roses On those that flower in a single flush on short

stems produced on a framework of older stems, remove up to one-third of the oldest stems, cutting back to a younger sideshoot near to the base after flowering in midsummer.

Repeat-flowering climbing roses Prune climbers that flower throughout the summer while dormant in winter. Cut back flowered sideshoots to a couple of buds.

Rambler roses Prune directly after flowering. Cut back old stems to a younger sideshoot lower down. If there are new, vigorous shoots coming from the base, cut out one old, exhausted, stem for each new shoot.

Shrubs, such as *Hydrangea paniculata,* that flower from midsummer onwards on growth produced that season should be pruned during early spring. The new shoots will then flower. You can either prune out one stem in three, or, for the most dramatic displays, cut back all the old growth to an outward-facing bud.

Pruning for foliage

Importantly in shady gardens, you will get bigger and more colourful leaves and stems from deciduous foliage shrubs, such as cornus, rubus and salix, by pruning them hard during early spring. Simply remove all the previous year's growth, cutting each stem back to an outward-facing bud to form a framework of stems near ground level. If this seems too drastic, use the one-stem-in-three pruning method instead.

Pruning clematis

Pruning clematis is slightly complicated, as the varieties fall into three distinct pruning groups, each requiring different treatment.

GROUP 1
includes the spring-flowering types, such as varieties of *Clematis alpina, C. armandii, C. macropetala* and *C. montana,* which have relatively dainty blooms that are produced on old wood. Most are well behaved and require little pruning other than the removal of dead or damaged stems after flowering.

GROUP 2
includes popular varieties such as 'Daniel Deronda', 'Ernest Markham', 'Lasurstern', 'Nelly Moser, 'Vyvyan Pennell' and 'The President', which all flower on old wood and again on new wood later in the summer. Little routine pruning is required, although you can encourage two distinct flowering flushes by relay pruning – cutting half the stems back to a pair of buds near ground level after flowering.

GROUP 3
includes most of the late-flowering hybrids, such as 'Abundance', 'Bill MacKenzie', 'Duchess of Albany', 'Etoile Violette', 'Jackmanii', 'Perle d'Azur' and 'Ville de Lyon', which need to be pruned routinely to keep them flowering well. During early spring, cut back all the stems to a pair of healthy buds between knee and waist height.

Many evergreen shrubs, including conifers (*see* opposite), do not respond at all well to hard pruning. Instead, keep them in shape and under control by trimming back wayward stems with secateurs several times a year. Try to avoid cutting back into leafless, woody stems, since these can be reluctant to resprout.

Pruning conifers

Most conifers do not need pruning. However, if the light levels are not even they can become misshapen and start leaning towards the brighter side, so pruning can be worthwhile. Also, the growth of conifers in shade can open up, becoming less dense. This can to some extent be corrected by annual trimming any time from

Honeysuckle and wisteria

Honeysuckles can be divided into two pruning groups, depending on the type of growth. If the climber bears its flowers in pairs on new growth produced in spring, such as *Lonicera japonica* varieties, it can be cut back during the winter or in early spring.

Varieties that produce their flowers in whorls on old wood should be pruned after flowering, with the spent flowered shoots cut back to a newer sideshoot lower down.

Wisteria produces abundant growth that needs trimming to keep it in check. The easiest way to do that is to prune it in two stages: in late summer, cutting back new, whippy growth to five or six leaves; and in winter, cutting the same stumps back to two or three buds

① **Summer trim** Cut back whippy stems to six leaves.
② **Winter prune** Cut back resulting stubs to two or three buds.

autumn to midwinter. To restrict the size of spreading or ground-hugging conifers, cut back individual branches to a younger side shoot. Making the cuts underneath green foliage will help disguise the pruning. Remove two or three branches each year, aiming to maintain the plant's overall shape. Upright-growing or shrubby conifers can be kept small by trimming regularly, as you would a hedge, but in this case follow the natural outline of the conifer.

Cutting back perennials

In a shady garden, herbaceous perennials that die back to ground level each winter are worth cutting back in autumn to keep the borders looking neat. The lankier growth often put on in shade will need clearing once the frost has blackened the foliage during late autumn.

Exceptions to this rule are perennials with attractive seedheads,

Clematis should be cut back to a healthy pair of buds. The timing and method used will depend on the variety being tackled (*see* box, page 54).

such as sedums, and borderline hardy perennials, which should have their top-growth left in situ until early spring. Alternatively, clear the border and protect vulnerable plants with an insulating layer of autumn leaves or other dry material.

Keeping grasses tidy

Ornamental grasses also benefit from an annual trim. Reinvigorate older plants in shade that have lost their sparkle by cutting them back hard during early spring, which will stimulate a vigorous regrowth of brightly coloured leaves.

In shade, more grasses will tend to collapse by late autumn and these should be trimmed before mid-winter, while shorter and sturdier varieties of deschampsia, miscanthus and stipa can be left until late winter, when all of last year's stems and dead leaves can be removed.

Winter protection

All hardy plants are vulnerable to winter wet and cold during their first couple of years after planting, and these damaging effects are exacerbated by chilly winds. It's tempting to grow more borderline

Plants in containers are particularly vulnerable to winter cold, so insulate the roots by wrapping the pot with bubble polythene. Then insulate the top growth with a double layer of garden fleece.

hardy plants in a sheltered, shady garden, where there is plenty of protection from wind. These plants will appreciate protection during the winter months by wrapping them up in autumn and removing the covering in spring. A few will regrow from below ground even if the top is killed by frost, so protect their root areas too. Use a 15cm (6in) deep insulating mulch of dry leaves, straw – or even piles of hedge trimmings.

Cold-susceptible climbers and wall shrubs can be insulated with a double layer of garden fleece, or a sheet of fine-mesh netting stuffed with insulating material.

Some bulbs such as tuberous begonias are not frost hardy and need to be lifted and stored in trays somewhere frost free.

Lawns in shade

Lawn grass and shade aren't good companions. As soon as the available sunlight is reduced, lawn grasses lose their evolutionary advantage of being able to out-compete most other non-woody plants.

As light levels drop, grass thins out and gets leggy and less vigorous. If it is then allowed to grow too long the problem is exacerbated, and in deep shade lawn grasses may die out completely. To promote the thickest possible sward in dappled shade, cut the grass little and often – setting the blades of the mower slightly higher than for the rest of the lawn.

Establishing a new lawn

Specially blended grass seed and turf have now been developed to cope with light shade. Under deciduous trees and shrubs the best time to sow or lay new turf is during the spring, before the leaf canopy has had a chance to fill out. Once the new grass reaches about 8cm (3in) trim it lightly, removing about 2cm (¾in). During the first season after sowing or laying slowly lower the cutting height of the mower to about 4cm (1½in), but never remove more than one-quarter of the height of the grass.

Maintaining a lawn

Grass growing in shade will struggle to get sufficient soil nutrients and moisture, so is usually sparse and slow growing. Increase the light levels if possible by thinning overhead foliage, and water at the first signs of drought. Spiking the turf in autumn and controlling any moss will also help (*see* page 57).

Improve uneven lawns by top-dressing the whole area with sieved topsoil or proprietary turf dressing, or dealing with lumps and bumps individually. To do this, make an H-shaped cut in the turf with a sharp spade. Starting in the middle of the 'H', undercut the top and bottom flaps and carefully peel back. Add or remove soil as necessary to rectify the

If you are planning a new lawn for a shady site, choose grasses that will tolerate low light conditions.

problem before replacing the flaps and firming well. You may have to fill any gaps with a 50:50 mixture of sieved topsoil and sharp sand.

Bare patches caused by heavy wear can be reseeded (*see* box below). Consider protecting the lawn in the future by installing stepping stones or laying heavy-duty plastic mesh pegged down before reseeding.

Reseeding

To reseed a section of lawn, scratch the surface using a soil rake, or prick it with the tines of a fork to gently loosen the soil.

Scatter a general fertilizer at the recommended rate and sow with a shade-tolerant grass-seed mix. Use about 20g (1oz) per square metre for thin patches and 35g (1½oz) per square metre for areas that are completely bare. Mix into the soil with the rake and firm lightly before watering with a can fitted with a fine rose.

Protect from birds by covering with twiggy pea-sticks or fine netting.

HOW TO repair lawn edges

Lawn edges in dappled or partial shade where the soil tends to remain moist are vulnerable to damage long after the rest of the lawn has dried and is usable. In these circumstances, installing a permanent lawn edge such as a proprietary plastic edging, or framing the lawn with a mowing strip of bricks, will protect it. Broken edges can be repaired by recutting the whole edge with a half-moon edging iron or a straight-edged border spade. Repair short runs of broken edge as follows.

1 Cut out a square of turf that includes the damaged area, carefully undercutting it with a spade.

2 Turn the turf through 180 degrees so that the damaged area is within the lawn, and fill the hole with good-quality topsoil before feeding and reseeding.

Moss and algae

Moss and algae are both primitive plants that thrive in inhospitable places where nothing else will grow. They are largely confined to lawns and uncultivated shady areas, including steps, paving and decking.

Dealing with lawn moss

Spongy lawn surfaces that are easily indented with footprints are a sure sign of a heavy infestation of lawn moss. Moss can be controlled with proprietary lawn mosskillers, or sand containing iron sulphate, but the effect will be short-lived unless you tackle the underlying causes of compaction and poor drainage by spiking and remove any unhealthy build up of thatch by scarifying. To reduce the shade – one of the chief reasons for a mossy lawn – prune back as many overhanging branches as possible (*see* pages 22–3).

If you want to avoid using chemicals, try raking the moss out. It's hard work, but hiring a powered lawnraker will make life a lot easier.

Algae and liverworts

Algae can grow almost anywhere, living off nutrients gleaned from the rain and wind-blown dust particles. It forms a thin, slimy, green or brown film and will thrive in damp, sheltered corners that get no sunlight. This is only really a problem on surfaces underfoot, where it can be hazardous. In some instances – on statues, for example – algae is not unattractive and gives a pleasing, weathered effect.

On shady lawns, algae can form greenish, jelly-like lumps on the surface, and liverworts – strange, ear-shaped, leaf-like growths – will cover any bare soil. Both these plants are easily controlled using lawn mosskiller, but the causes, such as very acid soil or poor drainage, will have to be sorted out to prevent the problem from reappearing.

① Algae will soon cover any hard surface in damp shade. On larger areas you may want to use a proprietary cleaner.
② Rake out untreated moss from the lawn and use it to line hanging baskets.

A mossy glade

Moss is invaluable for filling sunless gaps with a carpet of emerald green that lasts all year round. It will be practically maintenance-free once established, because few weeds will be able to survive. Any that do can be pulled by hand or treated with a selective weedkiller that doesn't harm moss. Different varieties of moss can be bought at specialist nurseries.

Another way of achieving the same effect as moss is to use very low-growing, small-leaved plants such as *Soleirolia soleirolii*, which are often available in the house plant section of garden centres. But watch out – these are invasive and almost impossible to get rid of.

Watering and feeding

Shady gardens may not need watering as much as sunny ones, so it is easy to forget the critical areas that do. If you have limited time, concentrate your efforts on plants in drought-prone borders next to walls and in dry spots under trees and next to hedges, especially near evergreens. Containers and any new plants need a lot of attention too, of course.

Watering

Getting watering right in shade is sometimes more difficult than elsewhere because requirements can vary so much from area to area. Plants in soil that remains moist may not need watering at all, while new plants in dry shady spots will need watering as often as container plants on a sunny patio. Obviously, on light, free-draining soils watering is more critical and shortages become more acute more quickly. However, even here, once garden plants are well established most won't need watering at all.

Don't be tempted to water little and often – in this way, only the surface layer of the soil or compost gets wet and this encourages surface rooting, which makes the plants more susceptible to drought.

Watering methods

Watering plants by hand is an ideal way of winding down on a summer's evening. It also provides an opportunity to check for the first signs of pest or disease on neighbouring plants, to reflect on how well different combinations of plants are working together, and to make a mental note of jobs to do.

Using a watering can with a fine rose is all right if you've got just a few pots and seedlings to care for, but if your watering needs are more extensive you will need to invest in a hosepipe, preferably on a reel fitted next to an outside tap.

Automatic watering

This can be a practical solution to getting plants established in dry shady areas. Lay out networks of micro-bore tubing delivering drips of water at a steady pace where required

and make the whole system automatic by fitting a watering computer or timer to the delivery pipe or the outside tap supplying the water. This doesn't mean you can rest on your laurels, however, since these systems need regular checks to sort out blockages and other problems.

Feeding

Plants that run short of essential nutrients grow more slowly, flower less freely, and become vulnerable to pest and disease attack. Although

The key to successful watering is to apply it only where and when it is needed – and in sufficient quantity: soak the whole rootball each time you water.

Fit water butts to all available downpipes to make use of valuable rainwater.

Insert a bottomless, upturned plastic water bottle alongside a new shrub in dry shade to help make watering easier.

most plants in shady gardens don't require routine feeding once established, those in the most demanding areas, such as at the foot of a hedge or under a tree, will benefit from an annual boost each spring by applying a balanced general fertilizer. Some floriferous shrubs, such as roses, produce better displays if given a high-potash feed during spring and again in early summer.

It is worth bearing in mind that different types of soil vary in the amount of soil nutrients they hold on to. For example, a shady garden with heavy soil will retain a considerable amount of essential nutrients and slowly release them for the plants to absorb. A shady spot with free-draining sandy soil, on the other hand, will have the nutrients quickly washed out so that they are of no benefit to the plants. Here, annual supplementary feeding will be far more worthwhile.

Container-grown plants need regular feeding. One option is to add a slow-release fertilizer to the compost at planting time. This will gradually release the plant nutrients over several weeks or months, depending on the type used. The other option is to apply a liquid feed once a fortnight.

Understanding fertilizers

Fertilizers come in a variety of formulations and types that can be applied in different ways. There are organic (made from plant or animal derivatives) fertilizers and inorganic (chemical) fertilizers. Both need to be used in damp soil. Organic fertilizers are less prone to leaching, and do not harm soil-borne organisms, contaminate waterways or need to be measured quite so precisely as inorganic fertilizers.

The three major nutrients required by plants are nitrogen (N), phosphorus (P) and potassium (K), and the proportion of each in a fertilizer determines the sort of growth it will promote. Look on the packet to find out the ratio. Fertilizers also usually contain trace elements, including calcium, magnesium and sulphur. Some are formulated for a specific purpose, such as lawn feed-and-weed.

Nitrogen (N) encourages strong leafy growth.

Phosphorus (P) produces healthy roots and ripening.

Potassium (K) promotes flowering and fruit production.

Many plants benefit from an annual feed to keep them growing vigorously. Choose a general-purpose fertilizer such as Growmore (inorganic) or blood, fish and bone (organic). Plants that are competing for nutrients with larger neighbours will need feeding routinely.

Weeds

Weeds are as much of a nuisance in a shady garden as in any other. Most common weeds will grow in shade, given the opportunity, but those that hail from hedgerows and woodland edges, such as nettles and bindweed, will be best adapted and prove the most difficult to tackle. In dry shade, few weeds will grow. Weeds can be divided into two camps: annuals, such as groundsel and chickweed; and perennials, like dock and thistle.

Prevention

You can prevent weeds from gaining a foothold in your garden by covering up all the bare soil with weed-smothering ground-cover plants (*see* pages 99–104) and spreading mulches. Between well-established shrubs and trees in shade, where there are no bulbs or perennials, you can apply a special chemical to inhibit the germination of weed seeds. Proprietary chemicals formulated to control weeds between paving slabs and on gravel paths and driveways are also available.

Control

Annual weeds are easy to control by routine hoeing or hand weeding. Perennial weeds need to be removed with their roots intact otherwise they are likely to regrow. Some, such as dandelions, have carrot-like taproots that can be difficult to pull up, while others, such as bindweed, have brittle, shoelace-like roots that are nigh on impossible to remove without breaking. Perennial weeds are best thrown in the garden-waste recycling bin.

You can also control weeds by using a contact or systemic chemical weedkiller. The former affects only the parts of the plant it comes into direct contact with, whereas the latter is transported internally around the weed and destroys every part. Individual weeds can be controlled using a dab-on spot-treatment applicator, while larger areas can be tackled using a ready-

The key to controlling dandelions is to cut off the flower heads before they produce their seed 'clocks'.

to-use sprayer, or you can buy the undiluted chemical and mix it yourself in a pressure sprayer. Protect ornamental plants in shade with plastic sheeting and don't remove it until the spray is dry.

Lawns in shade often grow sparsely and are more easily colonized by lawn weeds. These can be removed by hand using an old kitchen knife, or treated with a special lawn weedkiller. There are combined treatments for moss if this is a problem too.

Neglected areas devoid of ornamental plants can be hand weeded, treated with a chemical weedkiller, or cleared of vegetation and covered with thick black polythene, or an old piece of carpet, for a few years until the weeds are smothered into submission. Bear in mind that really tough weeds, such as bramble, may take several seasons to eradicate completely.

If small, hoed-up weed seedlings can be left on the surface in dry shade, but in damp areas they are best collected up and put on the compost heap.

Six problem weeds in shade

① BRAMBLE

Established clumps of this perennial weed spread via arching, thorny stems that root at their tips, forming an impenetrable thicket.

Control Cut back and dig out rooted shoots. Cut back top-growth and treat any new growth with a suitable systemic weedkiller, or torch it with a flame gun.

② BINDWEED

This pernicious perennial climber spreads by creeping roots that may run more than 60cm (2ft) deep. It is very difficult to remove and can take over borders and shrubberies.

Control Cut back and stake with a cane for regrowth to clambr up. Once plenty of growth has been made, slip out the cane and place the shoots in a polythene bag. Spray a suitable systemic weedkiller inside the bag so that no spray can escape and leave until dry.

③ CLEAVERS

This annual 'sticky-stemmed' weed quickly scrambles through herbaceous borders in shade. Sets seed freely.

Control Brittle stems break easily, so trace stems back carefully to their roots, before the sticky seeds develop, and pull out by hand.

④ GROUND ELDER

Commonly found in shady herbaceous borders, this perennial weed spreads by shallow, underground stems. It will also flower and set seed.

Control Regular weeding will help reduce the problem, but to solve it you will have to dig up all the ornamental plants and remove every scrap of weed root from the soil. Alternatively, cut back top-growth and treat any new growth with a suitable systemic weedkiller.

⑤ JAPANESE KNOTWEED

This perennial garden escape, which thrives in shady gardens, is now a serious environmental problem and is classified as controlled waste in the UK.

Control Bamboo-like stems reach 3m (10ft) and are tough to chop, and the deep roots are nearly impossible to dig out. Spray flowering top-growth with a suitable systemic weedkiller in summer, but *not if the weed is near water*. A large clump is best dealt with by a specialist professional.

⑥ STINGING NETTLE

This is a useful weed for a wildlife garden, but a nuisance elsewhere. It is perennial, reaches 1.2m (4ft) and spreads by shallow, creeping stems. It also sets seed.

Control Straightforward to dig out as the thick yellow roots do not regrow.

Pests and diseases

Most pests and diseases will attack plants in sun or shade, so common pests like aphids and caterpillars are just as much of a nuisance in a shady garden. However, a few pests – particularly slugs and snails – and several diseases, notably leaf spots, downy mildew and rusts, seem to thrive in the moist, humid environment that a sheltered shady garden affords.

Prevention and control

You can go a long way to avoiding pest and disease problems in a shady garden by growing the right plants in the right place and making sure they are in good condition. A vigorous, contented specimen is much more likely to be able to shrug off any attacks without need for intervention.

Practise good garden hygiene, stay vigilant, and where possible choose disease-resistant varieties. If outbreaks are caught early they are much easier to deal with and ornamental plants will suffer less damage. All it takes is a walk around the garden of an evening, checking vulnerable plants. Individual pests such as slugs, snails and caterpillars can be picked off by hand and

disposed of. Small colonies of sap-sucking insects – often found in the soft growing tips of many vulnerable plants during late spring – are easy to rub out with finger and thumb.

If you are prepared to use chemicals, try to choose selective treatments that specifically tackle the pest in question.

Natural predators

One of the most effective ways of controlling pests is to encourage natural predators. You can do this by providing suitable habitats where they can feed, breed and set up home. Nectar-rich flowers, for example, will attract hoverflies and lacewings, which eat aphids, spider mites and other insect pests, while

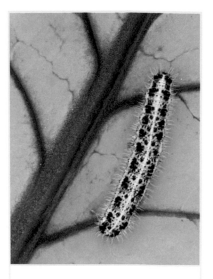

Caterpillars like shady conditions, so check plants in these areas regularly. In the vegetable garden, cabbage leaves are a favourite target.

piles of decomposing logs will provide a home for ground beetles and centipedes, which devour slugs, rootfly and vine weevils. A wildlife pond will soon be colonized by frogs and toads, who will scour your shady borders for slugs.

Living with slugs and snails

The constantly cool and moist conditions in a shady garden allow slugs and snails to move about at will devouring their favourite plants. Hosta, primula, ligularia and rodgersia are among their top targets, but they will also attack a wide variety of other plants.

If you have a slug problem in your garden, consider planting more slug-resistant plants such as *Alchemilla mollis* (lady's mantle), *Anemone x hybrida* and pulmonaria (lungwort), as well as any plants with hairy foliage (such as hardy geraniums).

If you want to grow hostas, try one of the varieties such as 'Sum and Substance' that have a reputation for being slug-resistant, or one of the thicker-leaved varieties such as 'Frances Williams', which seem to suffer rather less damage.

Ladybirds are voracious predators, feeding on aphids and other insects.

Pests and diseases to watch out for in shade

Leafspots These can affect a wide range of plants, especially those struggling in unsuitable conditions. Some, such as rhododendron leafspot, are specific to a particular type of plant. Few are serious and most don't warrant treatment. The exception is rose black spot, but this can often be avoided by growing black-spot resistant varieties.

Control Prevent carryover of the disease by clearing up diseased leaves before the new foliage emerges in spring. Mulching will also help prevent the spores in the soil infecting new foliage. Regular feeding and annual pruning to remove any black spot lesions and to encourage strong, new growth will help. If necessary, spray with a suitable rose fungicide at fortnightly intervals from the time new leaves emerge to mid-autumn.

Downy mildew

Grey or purplish mould appears on the under-sides of leaves with the upper surfaces developing yellow or brown areas. Badly diseased leaves may wither, but the plant itself may not be severely affected.

Powdery mildew

A white powdery deposit disfigures buds, leaves and stems.
Control Clear away diseased leaves.

Cut back all top growth on badly affected herbaceous plants. Improve air circulation by spacing plants and by pruning shrubs and climbers judiciously. Spray with a fungicide If necessary,

Rusts Rust-like spots on lower leaf surfaces can affect a wide range of plants. Many rust diseases are specific to certain types of plant and carry their name, such as fuchsia rust and hypericum rust.

Control Help prevent problems by improving air circulation – spacing out plants and thinning canopies by pruning. Pick off affected leaves and place in a garden-waste recycling bin. Tackle weeds that harbour the rust diseases, and rake up and dispose of diseased leaves in utumn.

Aphids These range from the small, green insects that attack roses to blackfly on beans and cherries, but also come in other colours, including yellow, pink, grey and brown. They suck sap, which weakens the host; excrete sticky honeydew, which often becomes colonized by black sooty mould that reduces the plant's ability to photosynthesize; spread viruses; and inject toxins into the leaf tissue, causing leaves to distort and blister.
Control Squash small colonies

between finger and thumb or dislodge with a powerful jet of water from a hose. Encourage natural predators. Treat large colonies with a suitable insecticide that won't kill other insects.

Caterpillars

The larvae of many species of butterflies and moths can attack plants in shady gardens. Angle shades, brown tail, buff-tip, hawthorn webber, lackey moth, small ermine and tortrix caterpillars are a few.
Control Pick off individual caterpillars – those protected by webbing can be squashed, or colonies can be cut out with the branch they are eating. If the problem is widespread, spray on a biological control or use a contact insecticide.

Slugs and snails

Moist, shady areas are the perfect environment for these soft-bodied pests. Look out for shredded and nibbled leaves and slime trails.

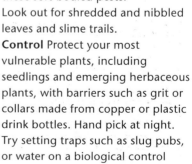

Control Protect your most vulnerable plants, including seedlings and emerging herbaceous plants, with barriers such as grit or collars made from copper or plastic drink bottles. Hand pick at night. Try setting traps such as slug pubs, or water on a biological control containing nematodes. Avoid using slug pellets, which can harm wildlife and pets.

Propagation

Raising your own plants from scratch is great fun and can save a lot of money. In a shady garden, it is likely you will need a lot of ground-cover plants, or you might want to propagate a new hedge or raise bedding plants to define the edge of a shady border. There are many ways of propagating plants, including sowing seed, taking cuttings, dividing clumps and layering individual branches.

Sowing seed

You can sow seed direct outside into prepared soil, but in a shady garden it is often more successful to sow in pots or trays where the perfect environment can be maintained. If you want to raise tender plants from seed to provide bedding displays, start them off in a thermostatically controlled propagator, indoors or in the greenhouse.

Different seeds require different temperatures and light conditions to germinate (these may be given on the packet). To make germination more reliable, you can buy primed, chitted or pre-germinated seed from some specialist suppliers. Others offer coated or pelleted seed, enabling you to space seeds more accurately and eliminate pricking out and thinning seedlings later on.

Some plants, such as lobelias and begonias, produce tiny seed that's no bigger than dust particles. You can make these easier to handle by adding dry silver sand to the packet to effectively 'dilute' the seed before you sow. The sand will also show up against the dark compost.

Raising seedlings

It is important to keep seedlings in the right conditions and not allow them to become overcrowded or run short of water. Prick out as soon as they are large enough to handle, spacing them into prepared cellular trays filled with fresh compost. Hold seedlings by their leaf and support the roots with a dibber, pencil or plant label to transfer them. Never hold them by the stem.

Water seedlings from below by standing the container in a tray of water until the surface of the compost darkens. Keep them in a bright place out of direct sunlight, at the correct temperature, until they are large enough to plant out.

Softwood cuttings taken from perennials generally root easily. With tender plants, wait until late summer.

Taking cuttings

There are several ways of taking cuttings – from stem, leafbud and root. Most shade-tolerant plants can be successfully propagated from stem cuttings. There are three main types: softwood, usually taken in late spring and early summer from new, fleshy growth; semi-ripe, taken in midsummer just as the new stems are turning woody at the base; and hardwood, taken in autumn and winter when the new wood has ripened fully.

Plants that are reluctant to grow from stem cuttings can be usually be propagated from root cuttings, and a few are more suited to the leafbud method. *See* box, page 67.

Softwood cuttings These can be taken any time while the plant is actively growing. Select a healthy, non-flowering sideshoot and trim it below a leaf joint, then remove the lower leaves and soft tip so that the cutting is about 5–8cm (2–3in) long.

In spring, you can also take basal cuttings, using new shoots as they

emerge from the base. Use a sharp knife to remove a 5–8cm (2–3in) long cutting where it joins the base.

Insert softwood cuttings around the edge of a pot filled with fresh cuttings compost and cover with a clear polythene bag secured with an elastic band. Place in a warm, well-lit position out of direct sunlight.

Prevent softwood cuttings from wilting by covering the pot with a clear polythene bag: inflate the bag or support it with twigs to keep it clear of the delicate leaves and stems.

Semi-ripe cuttings

These are young shoots that are just starting to turn brown and woody. They are best taken in mid- to late summer as the growth begins to harden on the current season's shoots. Semi-ripe cuttings are slightly tougher than softwood ones, so are less likely to wilt, but they will take longer to root. Many shrubs, such as camellia, root well when taken this way.

Leafbud cuttings

Some shade-loving plants, notably camellia, clematis, honeysuckle and mahonia, are easier to propagate from leafbud cuttings. Choose a piece of stem with a plump bud in the junction between the main stem and a leaf stalk and trim it just above the leaf joint and again a few centimetres below it, without damaging the bud. Insert the cutting up to the bud in a pot filled with fresh compost. Do not use hormone rooting powder on leafbud cuttings.

Hardwood cuttings

Although it is often recommended that you take these cuttings any time the plant is dormant, success rates are greater in autumn just after leaf fall. Some evergreens, such as privet, can be propagated from hardwood cuttings too. In this case, leave just the top few leaves on the cutting and trim away the remainder. *See* How to, below.

Root cuttings

If you want a lot of cuttings lift the plant and shake off the soil before plunging in a bucket of water to clean the roots. Cut off lengths of fleshy root (about pencil thickness if possible), trimming them to about 5cm (2in). Make a straight cut nearest the plant

HOW TO take hardwood cuttings

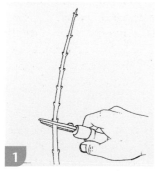

1 Using secateurs, remove a length of healthy stem from the current year's growth. Make a straight cut. If there are sideshoots present, trim them off.

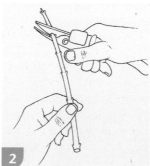

2 Trim the top of the shoot, making a sloping cut just above a bud. The cutting should be about 20cm (8in) long. Dip the base in hormone rooting powder.

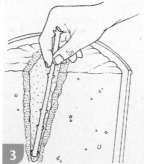

3 Fill a pot with free-draining cutting compost and moisten the compost well. Make a small slit trench in the compost. Insert the cutting into the trench, base first, leaving only the top third of the cutting showing above the surface.

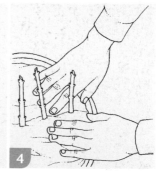

4 Continue inserting cuttings, then close the trench by firming compost around it. Water well and stand the pot in a well-lit, frost-free, sheltered spot outside over winter. Once the cuttings have rooted, pot them up separately.

Well-established hostas can be propagated by splitting a clump so that there is at least one good swollen bud and plenty of roots on each section. To get a lot of hostas quickly, for a new area of shady ground cover, for example, you may want to try a trick-of-the-trade called 'topping'.

■ Lift the parent plant while dormant, between November and February, then clean and trim the roots.

■ Divide into sections with plump buds.

■ Cut off the top third of each bud, then make a vertical, cross-shaped cut in the top of the stub – cutting right down to the woody base.

■ Dust with fungicide, then plant the prepared sections shallowly and cover with compost or pot them up.

■ By early summer they should have developed plenty of new buds around the cuts. The sections can then be cut up, so that there is a plump bud and roots on each.

■ Dust with fungicide, once again, before planting or potting up.

Layering

A few shade-loving shrubs and climbers that aren't easily propagated from cuttings or seed can be successfully rooted by layering. This encourages selected flexible stems to produce roots while still attached to the parent plant. There are several variations of this technique. Simple layering is the easiest (*see* How to, page 67).

Some plants need further encouragement to root by wounding the underground portion of the shoot and dusting it with hormone rooting powder before burying. Most shrubs and climbers will have rooted within six months, but a few can take 18 months or more.

Serpentine layering can be used on climbers with long, pliable stems, such as clematis. Follow the steps for simple layering, but peg down more nodes along the rest of the stem, looping sections above soil level.

and a slanted cut furthest away, so that you know which way up to insert the cuttings. If the roots are thin, make the cuttings about 8cm (3in) long. Place the prepared cuttings in a polythene bag with a little fungicidal powder and shake. Insert large cuttings vertically with their straight cut ends just showing above the compost. Thin root cuttings should be laid horizontally on the surface and lightly covered with compost.

Division

Several shade-loving shrubs and most perennials can be propagated by dividing the crown (a tightly knit lump of stem bases and roots).

The best time to carry out division is directly after flowering, but it's really only practical to divide plants either during early spring before new shoots emerge, or in autumn after the top-growth can be cut back. Plants that are borderline-hardy are best divided in spring after the worst winter weather is over.

Most perennials can be divided every three to five years, which keeps them vigorous and flowering well. However a few, such as hellebores, resent having their roots disturbed and should be left until the flowering performance of the clump starts to decline.

HOW TO propagate by division

Cut back the perennial to be divided and water thoroughly at least 24 hours beforehand.

Lay a polythene sheet in an open area near the plant – on the patio or lawn. Loosen the soil around the plant using a border fork and then lift the crown onto the plastic sheet.

Tease the crown apart, either by hand, a pair of garden forks pushed back-to-back, or, if very woody, by slicing into sections with a border spade. Make sure each clump has a portion of both shoots and roots, then discard the old, woody central part. Replant each section.

Thicket-forming shrubs that spread by rooting the tips of arching stems can be propagated by tip layering. Simply bury the shoot tip in the soil in late spring, and lift in autumn.

Shrubs with flexible, woody stems, such as dogwoods and acers, can be propagated by French layering. In this case, peg the stems horizontally before the buds break. When the new sideshoots are about 5cm (2in) long, bury the horizontal stems, leaving the tips of the sideshoots above soil level. These can be earthed-up as they grow and root. Once 15cm (6in) tall, they can be separated from the parent.

Propagating methods for shade-tolerant plants

SEED
Alchemilla, anemone, aquilegia, birch, campanula, callicarpa, cotoneaster, digitalis, euphorbia, geranium, hellebore, hosta, liriope, lobelia, lupin, lysimachia, penstemon, primula, pulmonaria, rodgersia and tellima.

SOFTWOOD CUTTINGS
Campanula, dicentra, euphorbia, lupin and penstemon.

SEMI-RIPE CUTTINGS
Berberis, chaenomeles, choisya, escallonia, euonymus, fatsia, gaultheria, hebe, hydrangea, ivy, myrtus, philadelphus, photinia, pyracantha, rhododendron, viburnum and vinca.

HARDWOOD CUTTINGS
Berberis, buxus, clematis, cornus, cotoneaster, deutzia, elaeagnus, escallonia, forsythia, garrya, griselinia, honeysuckle, jasmine, kerria, ligustrum, nandina, parthenocissus, salix, sambucus, sarcococca, skimmia, viburnum and weigela.

LEAFBUD CUTTINGS
Camellia, clematis, honeysuckle and mahonia.

ROOT CUTTINGS
Brunnera, chaenomeles, dicentra, phlox and primula.

DIVISION
Ajuga, alchemilla, anemone, aquilegia, aruncus, aster, astilbe, bergenia, campanula, convallaria, dicentra, digitalis, doronicum, euphorbia, geranium, gunnera, helleborus, hosta, hypericum, lamium, liriope, lobelia, lysimachia, peony, phlox, polemonium, polygonatum, primula, pulmonaria, rodgersia, ruscus, tellima and vinca.

LAYERING
Camellia, chimonanthus, clematis, cornus, daphne, hamamelis, ivy, magnolia, parthenocissus, pieris, rhododendron and viburnum.

Propagating hardy ferns

A few shade-loving hardy ferns, notably the maidenhair fern (*Adiantum*), can be lifted and divided like a perennial (*see* page 66). It is also possible to divide the lady fern (*Athyrium filix-femina*) if a side rhizome has sufficient roots, while *Polystichum* can be propagated from bulbils that form along the midrib on the underside of the fronds. The rest can be propagated from spores.

■ Collect ripe spores on a sheet of white paper and sow them like tiny seed on the surface of moist, fresh seed-sowing compost in a pot or seedtray.

■ Don't cover with compost, but place clingfilm over the pot to increase humidity after misting the spores with a hand sprayer.

■ Place in a propagator set at 15°C (60°F).

A mossy layer of germinated spores will form that can be 'pricked out' in small clumps into a fresh pot of compost. Mist regularly until the individual ferns grow large enough to be pricked out.

HOW TO propagate by layering

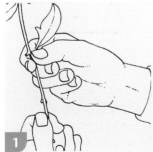

1 Select a strong, healthy, pliable low-growing shoot and strip off leaves about 20cm (8in) behind the growing tip.

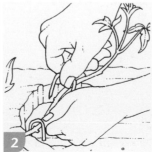

2 Pull the shoot down to ground level and bend it at right angles, about 20cm (8in) from the growing tip.

3 Prepare a planting hole at this point and peg the shoot down, tying the growing tip to a short bamboo cane so that it is held vertically out of the hole.

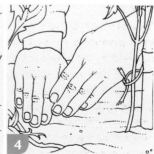

4 Fill in the hole and firm before watering thoroughly.

Plants for shade

Whatever type of shade you have in your garden you can rest assured there is no shortage of plants to choose from. The trick is to position them in conditions they will like. Apart from the degree of shade that a plant can tolerate, the most important considerations are whether the soil is acid or alkaline, and whether the area you're going to plant is dry or moist. To help you choose, the plants in this section are given symbols (*see* opposite) to indicate their tolerance of shade and their soil requirements.

Bulbs

After the bleakness of winter, there can be few more uplifting sights than that of early-flowering bulbs bursting from the frosty ground in early spring. Planting bulbs is one of the easiest ways to create a breathtaking spring or autumn display – and all for very little effort. Some bulbs are naturally adapted to shady or semi-shaded conditions, so they are the obvious choice for the shady garden.

Making choices

You should be able to find a bulb for just about any situation – in the shadow of walls and fences, in the dry soil under trees and between shrubs, and in boggy, shaded places next to ponds and streams. However, it's very easy to get carried away, especially in autumn when the garden centres are bursting with numerous varieties of spring-flowering bulbs, all promising spectacular results.

When you are planting the shady spots in the garden, it is important to remember that not all bulbs will grow in all types of shade and in all soils. For example, in moist (but not waterlogged) shade under trees you could try eranthis (winter aconite), grape hyacinth and the species daffodil *Narcissus cyclamineus*. But if the soil remains dry, snowdrops and bluebells are a better bet.

Next to walls, *Arum italicum* subsp. *italicum* 'Marmoratum' or *Cyclamen hederifolium* are good choices, and to light up permanently wet areas *Leucojum aestivum* or trilliums are usually good bets.

Some bulbs, especially summer-flowering ones such as lilies, require sunlight for at least part of the day in order to build sufficient reserves to flower reliably the following year.

Tulips crammed into pots can be placed wherever you need some early spring colour. Even a mixture of varieties can work well.

A few choices for moist shade

Anemone blanda
(wood anemone)

Arum italicum subsp. *italicum* 'Marmoratum' (lords and ladies)

Eranthis hyemalis
(winter aconite)

Erythronium dens-canis
(dog's-tooth violet)

Leucojum aestivum
(summer snowflake)

Leucojum vernum
(spring snowflake)

Narcissus cyclamineus
(species daffodil)

Trillium grandiflorum
(wake robin)

Moist and dry shade

Throughout this chapter a few plants have been picked out for their particular tolerance of moist and dry shade. These lists are not exhaustive, but they will help get you started.

A few choices for dry shade

Chionodoxa luciliae
(glory of the snow)

Colchicum speciosum

Cyclamen coum
(sow bread)

Galanthus nivalis
(common snowdrop)

Hyacinthoides non-scripta
(English bluebell)

Lilium martagon
(turkscap lily)

KEY to symbols

In this chapter the following symbols are used to indicate a plant's preferred growing conditions. Unless otherwise specified, plants are fully hardy. A rough idea is also given as to what each plant's height (H) and spread (S) might be at maturity. Plants in a blue-tinted box are especially recommended for their reliability and good value.

○ Prefers/tolerates an open, sunny site

◑ Prefers/tolerates some shade

● Prefers/tolerates full shade

❄ Will survive winter in a sheltered site

❀ Always needs protection from frost

◗ Prefers/tolerates moist soil

◊ Prefers/tolerates dry soil

⇊ Needs well-drained soil

pH↓ Needs/prefers acidic soil

pH↑ Needs/prefers alkaline soil

pH→ Needs/prefers neutral soil

🍂 Needs humus-rich soil

❖ Season of main interest (e.g. flowers, foliage, stems, berries)

Anemone blanda
Wood anemone
◯◐◗◌⛆ ❄️LATE WINTER TO LATE SPRING
H and S 15cm (6in)

This charming, spreading, tuberous perennial forms clumps of deeply lobed leaves and has daisy-like flowers in shades of deep blue to white. Perfect for naturalizing around the base of shrubs and in dappled shade under deciduous trees, it looks most dramatic when planted in bold drifts.

Chionodoxa luciliae
Glory of the snow
◯◐◗◌⛆ ⚌ ❄️SPRING
H 15cm (6in) **S** 3cm(1in)

This tiny bulbous perennial is one of the first to bloom after winter. When used en masse it produces a spellbinding carpet of starry blue flowers before the overhanging shrubs start to leaf up. It's ideal for naturalizing in dry, shady areas at the bottom of hedges and under deciduous shrubs.

Crocus tommasinianus
◯◐◗◌⛆ ⚌ ❄️LATE WINTER TO EARLY SPRING
H 10 (4in) **S** 3cm (1in)

This easy-to-grow shade-tolerant crocus comes in a range of flower hues from haunting, silvery lilac to warm, shade-piercing purple. Self-seeds readily and has needle-like grey-green leaves. Plant it at the base of a hedge or in partially shaded areas between shrubs and trees.

Arum italicum subsp. italicum
'Marmoratum' Lords and ladies
◯◐◗◌ ⚌ ❄️LATE WINTER TO SUMMER
H 30cm (12in) **S** 15cm (6in)

The clumps of cream-veined, arrow-shaped dark-green leaves form a late-winter carpet; during early summer greenish-white flower-like spathes appear, followed by spikes of attractive bright orange-red berries (poisonous). It provides long-lasting colour and interest in a shady border alongside a wall or fence, or under deciduous trees.

Colchicum speciosum
◯◐◗◌ ⚌ ❄️LATE SUMMER TO EARLY AUTUMN
H 18cm (7in) **S** 10cm (4in)

Elegant, goblet-shaped, bright pinkish-purple flowers with white throats and golden anthers shoot from bare soil in late summer. The glossy, leek-like foliage appears in spring. This is a good bulb for dry, shady borders along walls and at the bottom of hedges, as well as under specimen deciduous trees. Deep shade will restrict flowering. Good varieties: 'Album' (white flowers: shown above)

Cyclamen coum Sow bread
◐◗◌⛆ ⚌ ❄️LATE AUTUMN TO EARLY SPRING
H and S 10cm (4in)

This diminutive cyclamen forms a delightful carpet of kidney-shaped, silvered leaves, which are decorated with nodding carmine-red, pink or white flowers with rounded, upswept petals. It's good for lighting up areas of moist shade next to paths that don't get waterlogged and for planting between trees and shrubs, where it will tolerate dry soil.

Eranthis hyemalis Winter aconite

○ ◑ ♦ pH→ -pH↑ 🍂 ❖ LATE WINTER TO EARLY SPRING
H 8cm (3in) S 5cm (2in)

Light up damp, shady areas with these golden-yellow, buttercup-like flowers set off by decorative, deeply dissected ruffs of emerald-green foliage. This clump-forming perennial is a great woodland-edge or shady-stream plant.

Erythronium dens-canis

Dog's-tooth violet

○ ◑ ♦ ↕↕ 🍂 ❖ EARLY TO MID-SPRING
H 15cm (6in) S 10cm (4in)

Clumps of attractive grey-green leaves marbled with purple support dainty single white or pink flowers with prominent anthers. It works well for naturalizing in shady glades with moist soil that doesn't remain waterlogged. Good varieties: 'Lilac Wonder' (purple flowers); 'Pink Perfection' (pink flowers); 'White Splendour' (brown-centred white flowers)

Fritillaria meleagris

Snake's-head fritillary

○ ◑ ♦ 🍂 ❖ MID- TO LATE SPRING
H 30 (12in) S 8cm (3in)

With its intricately chequered, bell-shaped lanterns in shades of pink, purple and white that nod on slender stems over clumps of grey-green leaves, fritillaries look most effective planted en masse in damp, long grass under trees. Good varieties: 'Alba' (white flowers: shown above)

Galanthus nivalis

Common snowdrop

◑ ♦ ◊ pH→ -pH↑ 🍂 ❖ MID- TO LATE WINTER
H 20cm (8in) S 10cm (4in)

Wake up a shady garden with these tiny, sweetly scented white flowers. They look great planted in bold drifts naturalized in grass under deciduous trees, and are also good for lifting areas of dappled shade next to paths, between shrubs and trees and alongside fences where the ground doesn't get waterlogged.

Hyacinthoides non-scripta

English bluebell

◑ ♦ ◊ ↕↕ ❖ MID- TO LATE SPRING
H 40cm (16in) S 8cm (3in)

These clear-blue flowers steal the show in a woodland planting. English bluebells produce graceful spikes of scented, pendent bells from clumps of lance-shaped, dark-green leaves. It can be invasive in small gardens, but copes well with dry shade under deciduous trees and can be grown as a seasonal highlight on the shady side of a hedge.

Leucojum aestivum

Summer snowflake

○ ◑ ♦ pH→ -pH↑ 🍂
❖ MID-SPRING TO EARLY SUMMER
H 45cm (18in) S 8cm (3in)

A majestic, bulbous perennial producing upright, strap-shaped leaves and clusters of white, green-tipped, bell-shaped flowers with a faint, sweet fragrance reminiscent of Belgian chocolates. It's a good choice for naturalizing in shady glades with moist soil, alongside streams and in other wet areas.

Leucojum vernum Spring snowflake

○ ◑ ◔ ◊ ⁂ ❖EARLY TO MID-SPRING

H 30cm (12in) S 8cm (3in)

This is great for naturalizing in shady glades with moist soil that doesn't remain waterlogged. It has clusters of white, green-tipped, bell-shaped waxy flowers and upright, strap-shaped leaves.

Lilium martagon Turkscap lily

○ ◑ ◔ ◊ ⁞ ❖EARLY TO MIDSUMMER

H 1.5m (5ft) S 30cm (12in)

This easy-to-grow alpine bulb bears open spikes of up to 50 nodding, maroon-spotted purple flowers above clumps of dark-green leaves. The flowers have a rather unpleasant, pungent odour, though. It copes well with dry shade under deciduous trees and can be grown as a seasonal highlight on the shady side of a hedge.

Muscari armeniacum
Grape hyacinth

○ ◑ ⁞ ❖EARLY TO MID-SPRING

H 20cm (8in) S 5cm (2in)

The familiar grape hyacinth bears dense, grape-like, cone-shaped spikes of tiny bright-blue flowers above clumps of strap-shaped, fresh-green leaves. It is an ideal bulb for shady containers (use a gritty mixture of John Innes No. 2 compost) or for naturalizing under a deciduous specimen tree.

Narcissus cyclamineus
Species daffodil

○ ◑ ◔ ⁞ ❖EARLY TO MID-SPRING

H 20cm (8in) S 5cm (2in)

Ideal for shady containers or for naturalizing under a deciduous specimen tree, this delightful dwarf species has nodding, golden, narrow-waisted, long-trumpeted flowers with distinctive swept-back petals (rather like a cyclamen). It usually has one flower per stem.

Ornithogalum nutans
Star-of-Bethlehem

○ ◑ ⁞ ❖MID - TO LATE SPRING

H 25cm (10in) S 5cm (2in)

This bulb's nodding, silvery grey-green, funnel-shaped bluebell-like flowers add an intriguing, ghostly atmosphere to a shady glade. Plant in informal areas.

Trillium grandiflorum Wake robin

○ ◑ ◔ ⁞ ⁂ ❖MID-SPRING TO EARLY SUMMER

H 40 (16in) S 30cm (12in)

Exotic-looking, vigorous perennial that forms clumps of stalkless, distinctly veined, dark-green leaves with open, lily-like flowers. The puckered petals start out white and gradually fade to pink from mid-spring. This naturalizes well in areas of semi-shade between shrubs and in the dappled light under deciduous trees.

Perennials

Perennials – long-lived border plants that do not produce any woody growth – are an indispensable group for the shady garden. Most are herbaceous and die back in winter, resprouting from a crown or roots underground each spring. A few are evergreen and hold on to their foliage over winter until new shoots emerge in spring.

This is a very varied group of plants. Some are relatively short-lived and need replacing every few years, while others will grow and spread for a decade or more.

Most perennials flower for a few weeks (though some go on for a few months), generally during late spring or early summer. However, there are notable examples that bloom at other times of the year.

Adaptations and habit

Perennials are adapted to a range of conditions, many having evolved to grow in woodland, beside hedgerows and permanently shaded hillsides, or in canyons and crevices, making them an ideal choice for a garden with areas of shade – whatever the type. Some prefer moist, humus-rich soils, whereas others can cope quite well with drought and poor soils.

They have evolved a variety of growth habits, too, with some shooting skywards and others creeping along the ground. Plant breeders have added to the range, developing forms with variegated and coloured foliage as well as flowers in every colour.

Most perennials prefer direct sunlight for at least part of the day, so it is important to choose carefully when selecting plants for a shady site. In borders against north-facing walls and fences, for example, it is worth choosing late-emerging perennials that are not given a set-back by slow-to-warm soils.

Perennials can be used in many garden styles, from the carefree planting of cottage gardens to the more formal layouts of contemporary designs.

See also Ground cover, pages 99–104, for low-growing perennials.

Lupins come in all colours of the rainbow and make a lovely show in a partially shaded border, although they also cope well in full sun.

A few choices for dry shade

Acanthus mollis
(bear's breech)

Anemone × hybrida
(Japanese anemone)

Dicentra spectabilis
(bleeding heart)

Helleborus orientalis
(Lenten rose)

Ophiopogon planiscapus 'Nigrescens'
(black lilyturf)

Perennials for deep shade

Actaea matsumurae 'White Pearl'
(bugbane)

Anemone × hybrida
(Japanese anemone)

Hosta
(plantain lily)

Liriope muscari
(blue lilyturf)

Pulmonaria officinalis
(Jerusalem cowslip)

Tricyrtis hirta
(toad lily)

A few choices for moist shade

Astilbe chinensis var. *pumila*

Astrantia major
(masterwort)

Digitalis purpurea
(foxglove)

Gunnera manicata
(Chile rhubarb)

Hosta
(plantain lily)

Primula japonica
(Japanese primrose)

Primula vulgaris
(primrose)

Rodgersia pinnata

Thalictrum aquilegiifollium
(meadow rue)

Acanthus mollis Bear's breech
○ ◐ ◌ ◊ ⬍ ❖LATE SUMMER
H 1.5m (5ft) S 90cm (3ft)

An architectural beauty with towering, stiff spikes of purple-hooded, white or pink flowers above deeply lobed, glossy green leaves. This is perfect for adding height and drama to partially shaded borders and copes well with dry shade.

Actaea simplex 'Brunette'
Bugbane
◐ ◌ ◊ 🍂 ❖EARLY TO MID-AUTUMN
H 1.2 cm (4ft) S 60cm (2ft)

A relatively new introduction that produces clumps of lobed, deep purple-bronze leaves that throw up dramatic, pink-tinged white bottlebrush-like flowers in early autumn. Good as interest in the middle of a shady border just as other perennials are on the wane. Other good varieties: *A. matsumurae* 'White Pearl' (white flowers)

Anemone × hybrida
Japanese anemone
○ – ● ◌ ◊ 🍂 ❖LATE SUMMER TO MID-AUTUMN
H and S 1.5m (5ft)

The elegant, saucer-shaped pink or white blooms of this lovely anemone are borne on tall, wiry stems. They look their best in partial shade, but can tolerate full sun. This can be difficult to establish, but it is worth the effort and copes well with dry soil. Good varieties: 'Honorine Jobert' (pure white flowers: shown above); 'Queen Charlotte' (sugar-pink flowers)

Aquilegia Granny's bonnet
○ ◐ ◌ ◊ ⬍ ❖LATE SPRING TO EARLY SUMMER
H 60cm (2ft) S 30cm (12in)

Columbine forms mounds of ferny foliage, with elegant spurred flowers on upright, slender stems. There are varieties in virtually every colour. It is excellent for cutting. This looks good in a cottage-style planting or as part of a herbaceous border in partial shade. Good varieties: *A.* McKana Group (blue, yellow and pinky-red flowers); *A.* 'Red Star' (red flowers)

Aruncus dioicus Goat's beard
○ ◐ ◌ ◊ 🍂 ❖EARLY TO MIDSUMMER
H 2m (6ft) S 1.2m (4ft)

Grown for both its foliage and flowers, this lovely perennial produces masses of shaggy, creamy-white plumes above clumps of ferny foliage. Try it under trees, or alongside a stream or shady pond. Good varieties: *A. dioicus* 'Glasnevin' (shown above)

Aster 'Little Carlow' Aster
◐ ◌ ◊ ⬍ ❖LATE SUMMER TO MID-AUTUMN
H 90cm (3ft) S 45cm (18in)

Most asters love full sun, but this little beauty will produce masses of cheerful, violet-blue daisies with bright-yellow centres from late summer to mid-autumn in partial shade. Ideal for giving shady borders a late-season fillip.

Astilbe chinensis var. pumila
○ ◐ ● ◌ 🌿 ❖ LATE SUMMER TO EARLY AUTUMN
H 25cm (10in) S 20cm (8in)

A compact astilbe producing mounds of deeply cut, red-tinged leaves that give rise to dramatic, pinky-purple feathery plumes. This superb dwarf variety copes well with moist soil: plant it in bold drifts for a dramatic impact. Other good varieties: A. 'Amethyst' (lilac-pink plumes); A.'Deutschland' (pure white plumes)

Astrantia major Masterwort
○ ◐ ● ◌ ◌ 🌿 ❖ SUMMER
H 90cm (3ft) S 45cm (18in)

A cottage-garden favourite with clusters of pincushion-like flowers surrounded by a pink-tinted pale-green ruff held above toothed leaves. This is a useful filler in dappled shade, and it copes well with moist soil. Good varieties: A. major subsp. involucrata 'Shaggy' (white flowers with green-tipped white ruff: shown above)

Campanula lactiflora
○ ◐ ● ◌ ◌ pH→ -pH↑ ❖ SUMMER
H 1.5m (5ft) S 60cm (2ft)

Superb bell-like, slate-blue flowers are borne in large trusses above attractively toothed leaves. Ideal for brightening up and adding height to the middle of a lightly shaded border or for filling gaps further back. Although it can tolerate full sun, the flower colour is best appreciated and less likely to fade if planted in partial shade. Good varieties: 'Loddon Anna' (soft-lilac flowers); 'Prichard's Variety' (dark violet-blue flowers)

Dicentra spectabilis Bleeding heart
○ ◐ ● ◌ ◌ pH→ -pH↑ ❖ LATE SPRING TO EARLY SUMMER
H 1.2m (4ft) S 50cm (20in)

Dainty, rose-pink, locket-shaped flowers are produced in rows on arching stems above clumps of ferny, fresh-green leaves. This is a good component of partially shaded herbaceous borders, where it will help bridge the colour gap between spring and early-summer flowers, and it can also cope well with dry soil. Good varieties: 'Alba' (white flowers); D. 'Stuart Boothman' (deep-pink flowers, feathery blue-grey leaves)

Digitalis × mertonensis
Dusky foxglove
○ ◐ ● ◌ 🌿 ❖ EARLY TO MIDSUMMER
H 90cm (3ft) S 30cm (12in)

Raspberry-sorbet coloured, tubular flowers are produced on elegant, towering spires above attractively veined, dark-green leaves. This is a head-turner when planted in bold drifts in partial shade – perfect for adding height and colour towards the back of a border too.

Digitalis purpurea Foxglove
◐ ● ◌ 🌿 ❖ EARLY TO MIDSUMMER
H 2m (6ft) S 60cm (2ft)

The towering, slender spires of maroon-spotted, purple to deep-pink tubular flowers of this beautiful biennial light up moist, dappled shade. It's short-lived, but a useful woodland edge plant or in informal schemes, where it can self-seed freely. Good varieties: Excelsior Group (maroon-spotted pastels); 'Sutton's Apricot' (apricot-pink flowers: shown above)

Euphorbia wallichii
◐◐△ ❋EARLY TO MIDSUMMER
H 50cm (20in) S 30cm (12in)

Compact, clump-forming perennial with purple-edged, dark-green leaves with white veining. Its orange-yellow flowers help brighten up the front of a partially shaded mixed border.

Gentiana sino-ornata Gentian
◐◐ pH↓ ❋AUTUMN
H 10cm (4in) S 30cm (12in)

These intensely coloured gentian-blue flowers – trumpet shaped, with intricate stripes and a white throat – shine out from lance-shaped leaves. Grow this spreading semi-evergreen in clumps under deciduous trees, but the soil must be moist.

Geranium phaeum
Mourning widow
○◐◐ ❋LATE SPRING TO EARLY SUMMER
H 80cm (32in) S 45cm (18in)

Sultry, deep-purple flowers that look jet-black in dappled light are held on slender stems above mounds of purple-blotched, deeply lobed pale-green leaves. This is a glorious choice for damp, dappled shade, or for partially shaded borders. Good varieties: 'Album' (ghostly white flowers); var. *phaeum* 'Samobor' (purple-black flowers)

Geum 'Mrs J Bradshaw' Avens
○◐◐△ ❋LATE SPRING TO MIDSUMMER
H 60cm (2ft) S 45cm (18in)

Attractive rosettes of hairy, kidney-shaped leaves throw up branching stems of semi-double, bright scarlet flowers, giving a cheerful lift to partially shaded borders. Other good varieties: *G.* 'Lady Stratheden' (yellow semi-double flowers)

Gunnera manicata Chile rhubarb
○◐❀◗ ❋MIDSUMMER
H 2.5m (8ft) S 4m (13ft)

If you have a lake with room to spare, this stunning architectural beauty would make the perfect addition. Its emperor-sized, deeply lobed, dark-green rhubarb leaves – on thick, prickly stalks – can span 2m (6ft) or more. Club-like, brown flowers are followed by spherical red-green fruit. Humus-rich, permanently moist soil is essential, and you'll need to protect the crown from the cold.

Helleborus niger Christmas rose
◐◐△ pH→ -pH↑ ❋LATE WINTER TO MID-SPRING
H 30cm (12in) S 45cm (18in)

Seductive, pink-flushed, white, bowl-shaped flowers nod soulfully above clumps of leathery, dark-green leaves with toothed margins. Perfect for brightening the front of a partially shaded mixed border. Good varieties: 'Potter's Wheel' (large white flowers with green centres)

Helleborus orientalis Lenten rose
◐●◌◌ ‖ ❖pH→-pH↓ ❖LATE WINTER TO SPRING
H and S 45cm (18in)

The Lenten rose's lovely outward-facing, saucer-shaped flowers are white, pink or greenish-cream. Clumps of leathery, dark-green leaves are the perfect foil. They can cope with dry soil and are ideal between deciduous trees, where they will form a knee-deep ground cover.

Helleborus × sternii Hellebore
◐❄●◌◌ ‖ pH→-pH↓ ❖LATE WINTER TO MID-SPRING
H 35cm (14in) S 30cm (12in)

This beautiful cross between *H. argutifolius* and *H. lividus* produces purple-stained, creamy, bowl-shaped flowers above clumps of leathery, spiny-edged purplish-green leaves. Good varieties: Blackthorn Group (purple-tinted flowers on purple stems)

Hosta Plantain lily
○-●●◌◌ ‖ ❖LATE SPRING TO AUTUMN

Hostas are quintessential shade-lovers and look great anywhere in the garden – unless you've got slugs and snails! 'Sum and Substance' (shown above) claims resistance, however. These clump-forming, herbaceous perennials are characterized by lush foliage that's often attractively puckered, coloured or variegated, with spikes of summer flowers. They cope well with moist soil.

Hosta 'Big Daddy'
◐●●◌◌ ‖ ❖LATE SPRING TO AUTUMN
H 60cm (2ft) S 1m (3ft)

This atttractive hosta has large, puckered, blue-grey leaves, with greyish-white flowers. Other good varieties for deep shade: 'Blue Wedgwood', 'Francee', 'Ginko Craig', 'Ground Master', 'Halcyon', 'Honeybells', 'Patriot', 'Shade Fanfare'

Hosta 'Royal Standard'
○◐●◌◌ ‖ ❖LATE SPRING TO AUTUMN
H 60cm (2ft) S 1.2m (4ft)

'Royal Standard' has shiny, heart-shaped, veined, fresh-green leaves. Its slightly fragrant, trumpet-shaped white flowers are borne well above the foliage and open in the evening. Tolerates full sun as well as partial shade. Other good varieties for partial shade: 'Gold Edger'; 'Gold Standard '; 'Golden Tiara'; 'Ground Master'

Liriope muscari Blue lilyturf
○-●●◌◌ pH→-pH↓ ❖YEAR-ROUND
H 30cm (12in) S 45cm (18in)

Tough and resilient, this stout evergreen perennial forms miniature fountains of dark-green, strappy leaves that erupt with long-lasting, vibrant wands of deep-violet flowers during late summer and last through to late autumn. Very useful for providing interest late in the season and looks great planted in groups under deciduous trees, or can be used to front the border of a shrubbery.

Lupinus 'Chandelier' (Band of Nobles series) Lupin

○ ◑ ◐ ◌ ⇅ pH→-pH↓
❖ EARLY TO MIDSUMMER, EARLY AUTUMN
H 90cm (3ft) S 75cm (30in)

Dramatic spires of brilliant-yellow, pea-like flowers stand stiffly above clumps of palmate, fresh-green leaves. Dead-head to encourage a second flush of flowers. This is a good border filler, but taller forms may need staking in shade.

Lysichiton americanus
Yellow skunk cabbage

○ ◑ ◐ ◌ ❖ MID- TO LATE SUMMER
H 1m (40in) S 1.2m (4ft)

A magnificent architectural plant. Bright-yellow flower-like spathes emerge from bare soil, followed by glossy, dark-green leaves up to 1m (40in) long. Plant by a partially shaded pond or stream.

Lysimachia clethroides
Chinese loosestrife

○ ○ ◑ ◐ ◌ ⇅ ❖ MID- TO LATE SUMMER, AUTUMN
H 90cm (3ft) S 60cm (2ft)

Curved wands of tiny white flowers shoot clear of clumps of narrow, fresh-green leaves, and there's a bonus of red leaves in autumn. This is Ideal planted towards the back of a partially shaded border that has had plenty of well-rotted matter added to the soil.

Meconopsis betonicifolia
Himalayan blue poppy

◑ ◌ pH↓ ❖ EARLY SUMMER
H 1.2m (4ft) S 45cm (18in)

If proof were needed that blue flowers look most spectacular in shady gardens, look no further than these marvellous sky-blue, saucer-shaped blooms with golden stamens. Although a short-lived perennial, it does spread without intervention. It looks good in drifts in the dappled light under deciduous trees.

Omphalodes cappadocica
Navelwort

◑ ◌ ◌ ⇅ ❖ EARLY TO MID-SPRING
H 25cm (10in) S 40cm (16in)

Evergreen perennial that forms clumps of heart-shaped green leaves decorated by sprays of white-eyed, gentian-blue flowers. This is an excellent ground cover for partially shaded borders or skirting a woodland edge. Good varieties: 'Starry Eyes' (white-edged gentian-blue flowers: shown above); 'Lilac Mist' (lilac-blue flowers)

Ophiopogon planiscapus
'Nigrescens' Black lilyturf

○ ◑ ◐ ◌ ◌ pH→-pH↓ ❖ YEAR-ROUND
H 20cm (8in) S 30cm (12in)

The soot-black, grassy foliage of black lilyturf makes neat edging all year round. Spikes of bell-shaped, mauve flowers are followed by blue-black berries. Use in beds and borders (it can cope with dry soil), or as an unusual ground cover. For a striking effect, underplant with snowdrops in dappled shade.

Paeonia lactiflora Peony
○ ◑ ▲ ◊ ‖ ❖ EARLY TO MIDSUMMER
H 50cm (20in) S 70cm (28in)

This flamboyant herbaceous perennial is a superb specimen plant for the middle of a partially shaded border. Its showy, scented flowers appear above a hummock of handsome dark-green foliage. Good varieties: 'Bowl of Beauty' (cream-centred, pink-tinted red flowers); 'Bunker Hill' (bright-red ruffled double flowers); 'Duchesse de Nemours' (shown above)

Polygonatum × hybridum
Solomon's seal
◑ ▲ ◊ ‖ ❖ LATE SPRING TO EARLY SUMMER
H 1.5m S 30cm (12in)

Tubular, pendent, green-tipped white flowers dangle in clusters from elegant arching stems winged with fresh-green leaves. The scented flowers are followed by small, round, blue-black fruits. This is perfect for a cool, shady border or woodland-edge planting.

Primula japonica
Japanese primrose
◑ ▲ ◊ pH→ - pH↓ ❖ LATE SPRING TO EARLY SUMMER
H and S 45cm (18in)

Tiers of red, purple and white flowers are produced on fleshy stems above rosettes of fresh-green leaves. Good in moist shade. Good varieties: 'Miller's Crimson' (dark dusky-red flowers); 'Postford White' (orange-eyed white flowers)

Phlox paniculata Perennial phlox
○ ◑ ▲ ◊ ‖ MIDSUMMER TO MID-AUTUMN
H 90cm (3ft) S 1m (40in)

This vigorous, upright perennial produces trusses of scented flowers – usually pink, mauve or white. Use border-linking stakes to support the top-heavy flowers in exposed gardens. Ideal for a mixed or herbaceous border in light shade. Good varieties: 'Brigadier' (orange-red flowers); 'Norah Leigh' (pale-lilac flowers: shown above); 'Starfire' (crimson flowers)

Primula florindae Giant cowslip
◑ ▲ pH→ - pH↓ ❖ EARLY TO MIDSUMMER
H and S 90cm (3ft)

Pendent clusters of slender, fragrant, sulphur-yellow flowers are supported on fleshy stems above rosettes of toothed leaves. Plant in shady grass.

Primula vulgaris Primrose
◑ ▲ ❖ SPRING
H 25cm (10in) S 35cm (14in)

Charming, slightly fragrant clusters of lemon-yellow flowers nestle in rosettes of veined, fresh-green leaves. This copes well with moist soil and naturalizes well in partially shaded grassy areas or on the banks of a stream in dappled shade.

Pulmonaria officinalis
Jerusalem cowslip
◗●♦ ❖ EARLY TO MID-SPRING
H 25cm (10in) S 45cm (18in)

Pink flowers mature to reddish-violet and finally blue on this useful shade-lover. The clumps of white-spotted, fresh-green leaves are retained throughout the year and will lighten any partially shaded areas of the garden. Good varieties: Cambridge Blue Group (light-blue flowers); 'Sissinghurst White' (white flowers: shown above)

Pulmonaria rubra Lungwort
◗●♦ ❖ LATE WINTER TO LATE SPRING
H 40cm (16in) S 90cm (3ft)

This variety produces clusters of funnel-shaped, deep-red to pinkish-red flowers sporadically from late winter to late spring above matt, evergreen leaves. It's a useful, spreading plant for shady areas. Good varieties: 'Redstart' (coral-red flowers: shown above); 'Barfield Pink' (white-striped pink flowers)

Rodgersia pinnata
○◗●♦ ❖ MID- TO LATE SUMMER
H 1.2m (4ft) S 75cm (30in)

This bold, clump-forming perennial is grown for its deeply divided, crinkled dark-green leaves. Spikes of star-shaped, red, pink and creamy-white flowers come as a bonus, and the frosted spikes look great in winter too. Excellent next to partially shaded water. Good varieties: 'Elegans' (copper-tinted leaves, pink flowers); 'Maurice Mason' (shown above)

Thalictrum aquilegiifolium
Meadow rue
◗●♦ ❖ EARLY SUMMER TO EARLY AUTUMN
H 1m (40in) S 45cm (18in)

Vivid, pinkish-purple fluffy plumes are carried against a backdrop of ferny, light-green foliage. Good for adding dramatic colour interest to a partially shaded corner or as part of a lightly shaded glade, but may need supporting.

Tricyrtis hirta Toad lily
◗●🦋 ❖ LATE SUMMER TO MID-AUTUMN
H 80cm (32in) S 60cm (2ft)

Get up close and personal with this exotic beauty to really appreciate the intricate markings of its miniature sprays of white, purple-spotted flowers held on upright, rigid stems. The leaves are hairy and lance-shaped. This clump-forming perennial makes a perfect talking point for a sheltered, partially shaded border or woodland edge.

Zantedeschia aethiopica
'Crowborough' Arum lily
○◗●❄♦ ❖ LATE SPRING TO EARLY SUMMER
H 90cm (3ft) S 60cm (2ft)

Dramatic, snow-white, hood-shaped flowering spathes rise from lush clumps of arrow-shaped, glossy dark-green leaves. This looks very effective in moist, shady borders, bog gardens or near water features. Good varieties: Z. 'Black Pearl' (purple-black flowers); 'Green Goddess' (green-suffused white flowers)

Evergreen shrubs

If you choose the right varieties, evergreen shrubs will add year-round sparkle to the garden. You can make a collection of them, or combine them with deciduous shrubs and flowers to provide a continuously changing display.

Ilex x *altaclerensis* 'Lawsoniana' – a useful evergreen for winter interest with its luscious red berries and glossy, gold-splashed leaves.

In the shady border, evergreens can provide a foil for other plants as well as shelter for less hardy neighbours. They will add natural structure to the display, with variegated and coloured-leaved varieties brightening up darker areas by adding drama and a point of focus that lasts all year.

Seasonal interest

During the spring, some evergreen shrubs are so stunning when they come into flower that they dominate the scene. Bear in mind that several of the most spectacular, including camellias, azaleas and rhododendrons, require an acid soil to do well. However, in gardens with chalky (alkaline) soil you can always grow them in containers filled with ericaceous compost.

By the time summer arrives most evergreens will have melted into the background as flowering shrubs and perennials take centre stage in the garden.

Although few evergreens can match the fiery autumn displays of the best head-turning deciduous shrubs and climbers, in winter many evergreen shrubs really come into their own with colourful foliage, brilliant berries and resilient flowers providing most of the highlights in the winter garden as well as material for flower arrangers and food for native birds.

A few choices for shady containers

Aucuba japonica
(spotted laurel)

Fatsia japonica
(Japanese aralia)

Camellia

Choisya × *dewitteana* 'Aztec Pearl'
(Mexican orange blossom)

Hebe rakaiensis
(shrubby veronica)

Rhododendrons and evergreen azaleas

If you have acid soil, evergreen azaleas and rhododendrons make excellent shrubs for shady gardens. They are grown for their funnel-shaped spring flowers produced in trusses or clusters, some so densely packed they form giant balls of glorious colour against the dark-green, shiny leathery leaves.

Even in a small garden you can grow one of the newer dwarf hybrids. These include: 'Anah Kruschke' (reddish-purple); 'Cheer' (shell-pink marked with red); 'Dopey' (lustrous red); 'Honeymoon' (greenish-yellow with lime green); 'Patty Bee' (pale yellow). See also pages 87–8.

Evergreen shrubs for deep shade

Aucuba japonica
(spotted laurel)

Leucothoe fontanesiana
(switch ivy)

Mahonia japonica
(Japanese barberry)

Pachysandra terminalis
(Japanese spurge)

Prunus laurocerasus
(cherry laurel)

Prunus lusitanica
(Portugal laurel)

Sarcococca confusa
(Christmas box)

Sarcococca hookeriana var. *digyna*
(Christmas box)

Skimmia × *confusa* 'Kew Green'

Skimmia japonica
(Japanese skimmia)

Evergreen shrubs for acid shade

Camellia japonica
(common camellia)

Camellia × *williamsii*

Gaultheria mucronata
(boxberry)

Kalmia angustifolia f. *rubra*
(sheep laurel)

Kalmia latifolia
(calico bush)

Leucothoe fontanesiana
(switch ivy)

Pieris japonica
(lily-of-the-valley shrub)

Aucuba japonica Spotted laurel
○–●▲◊ ⫶⫶ ❖YEAR-ROUND
H and S 3m (10ft)

Tough and resilient, this laurel forms a dense mound of lustrous, dark-green leaves with toothed margins. Inconspicuous flowers are followed by red fruits on female plants. Perfect for inhospitable, shady areas between buildings and at the base of a north wall as it copes well with dry shade. It also makes an excellent hedge for urban or coastal areas. Good in containers too. Good varieties: 'Crotonifolia' (female, ivory-speckled leaves: shown above)

Azalea see *Rhododendron*

Berberis darwinii Barberry
○◐▲◊ ⫶⫶ ❖SPRING, AUTUMN
H and S 3m (10ft)

Superb, spiny barberry that bears loose clusters of burnt-orange flowers from mid- to late spring, followed by rounded, blue-purple berries in autumn. Vigorous and easy to grow, it is clothed in small, holly-like prickly foliage so makes an impenetrable, informal flowering hedge in partially shaded areas.

Berberis julianae
○◐▲◊ ⫶⫶ ❖LATE SPRING, AUTUMN
H and S 3m (10ft)

Very spiny, upright barberry that bears dense clusters of yellow, late-spring flowers, followed by purple-black berries. Useful as an informal, flowering hedge.

Berberis × *stenophylla*
○◐▲◊ ⫶⫶ ❖SPRING, AUTUMN
H 3m (10ft) S 5m (18ft)

Carefree, arching branches of spine-tipped leaves carry clusters of dark-yellow flowers from mid- to late spring. Rounded, bluish-purple fruits follow. Good varieties: 'Claret Cascade' (red shoots); 'Lemon Queen' (creamy-white)

Berberis verruculosa
○◐▲◊ ⫶⫶ ❖LATE SPRING, AUTUMN
H and S 1.5m (5ft)

A useful, compact shrub with spine-tipped leaves. It bears single, golden flowers on arching shoots, followed by glaucous, purple fruit. This is vigorous and easy to grow, and makes a neat specimen shrub in partially shaded areas.

Buxus sempervirens Common box
●▲◊ ⫶⫶ ❖YEAR-ROUND
H and S 5m (16ft)

Fabulous, dense, small-leaved shrub that's slow-growing, so can be clipped to form neat, low hedges or left to grow into conical shrubs. Good for providing formal edging or for filling gaps, or as a dense backdrop for traditional herbaceous borders. Good varieties: 'Elegantissima' (white-edged leaves)

Camellia japonica
Common camellia

◐◑ pH↓ 🌿 ❖ LATE WINTER TO EARLY SPRING
H 9m (30ft) S 8m (26ft)

A vigorous, domed shrub with spectacular single red flowers not unlike waterlilies. Grow this in partial shade anywhere in the garden, but avoid an east-facing spot as early-morning sun after frost will damage the flowers. Good varieties: 'Elegans' (anemone-shaped, dark rose-pink flowers: shown above); 'Lady Vansittart' (semi-double pink-flushed white flowers, spiny leaves); 'Nobilissima' (yellow-centred white peony-shaped flowers)

Camellia × williamsii

◐◑ pH↓ 🌿 ❖ MID- TO LATE SPRING
H 5m (16ft) S 3m (10ft)

Showy, waxy-looking white to dark-pink flowers are borne on this rounded shrub with lustrous leaves. Good varieties: 'Anticipation' (crimson flowers); 'Debbie' (rose-pink peony-shaped flowers); 'E. G. Waterhouse' (double pink flowers: shown above)

Choisya × dewitteana 'Aztec Pearl' Mexican orange blossom

○◐◑ ⬢ ⫴ ❖ LATE SPRING, EARLY AUTUMN
H and S 2.5m (8ft)

A lovely variety that bears fabulously scented, star-shaped, pink-tinged white flowers during late spring with a later flush in early autumn. Compact and easy to grow with neat, aromatic dark-green foliage, but needs shelter from severe winter weather. Just right for a mixed or shrub border in light shade.

Cordyline australis Cabbage palm

○◐◑ ❄ ⬢◐○ ⫴ ❖ YEAR-ROUND
H 10m (32ft) S 4m (13ft)

This exotic-looking fountain of sword-shaped leaves eventually grows into a palm-like tree. Use young specimens as accents in mixed borders in partial shade, or grow as a focal point in a container. Good varieties: 'Atropurpurea' (purple-flushed leaves); 'Red Star' (deep-red leaves); 'Torbay Dazzler' (cream-striped leaves: shown above)

Daphne bholua

○◐◑ ⬢ ⫴ 🌿 ❖ MID- TO LATE WINTER
H 4m (13ft) S 1.5m (5ft)

Clusters of pinkish-white flowers stand out against the lance-shaped, dark-green leaves of this sweetly scented, upright shrub. Fleshy black berries follow. Good for a mixed or shrub border in light shade, or plant next to a well-used shady path or entrance to appreciate the fragrance. Good varieties: 'Darjeeling' ; 'Jacqueline Postill' (purple-pink flowers: shown above)

Daphne odora 'Aureomarginata'

○◐◑ ❄ ⬢ ⫴ ❖ WINTER TO EARLY SPRING
H and S 1.5m (5ft)

A highly fragrant, rounded shrub with handsome, yellow-edged leaves. Clusters of sweetly scented reddish-purple winter flowers are followed by fleshy red berries. Use this in a mixed or shrub border, or plant next to a path or entrance for the fragrance. It prefers sun but tolerates light shade.

Elaeagnus × ebbingei Oleaster
○ ◐ ◖ ◊ ↕ ❖ SYEAR-ROUND
H and S 4m (13ft)

A versatile, shade-tolerant shrub with leathery, dark-green leaves that are silvery underneath. The inconspicuous, creamy, fragrant flowers appear from mid- to late autumn. Excellent informal hedging plant or filler shrub for light shade; the plain foliage is a good foil for other shade-tolerant flowers.

Fatsia japonica Japanese aralia
○ ◐ ❄ ◖ ◊ ↕ ❖ SYEAR-ROUND
H and S 4m (13ft)

Architectural shade-lover grown for its giant, fig-shaped, glossy evergreen leaves, which help reflect light into dark corners. From early to mid-autumn, large lollipop-clusters of creamy flowers are a bonus, followed by rounded, black fruit. This shrub looks really tough, but is actually only just frost hardy. It makes an excellent focal point in a shaded corner sheltered from cold winds.

Gaultheria mucronata (syn. Pernettya mucronata) Boxberry
○ ◐ ◖ pH↓ ❖ SUMMER, WINTER
H and S 1m (40in)

Boxberry is grown mainly for its clusters of marble-sized autumn and winter berries, which vary in colour from white to purple. Masses of pink-flushed white flowers from late spring to early summer are a bonus. You'll need to plant both male and female forms for a good crop of berries. Good varieties: 'Mulberry Wine' (female, red berries)

Hebe rakaiensis Shrubby veronica
○ ◐ ◖ ↕ pH→ -pH↑ ❖ SUMMER TO AUTUMN
H 1m (40in) S 1.2m (4ft)

This is a lovely, rounded shrub that's really tough and resilient. Frothy spikes of small white flowers appear from early to midsummer, standing proud of neat mounds of glossy leaves. Ideal for low hedges and for adding substance to mixed borders in light shade, and useful in oriental-style gardens, too.

Ilex × altaclerensis Holly
○ ◐ ◖ ↕ ❖ YEAR-ROUND
H 20m (64ft) S 15m (48ft)

Holly cross between *I. aquifolium* and *I. perado,* with lance-shaped, spiny, dark-green leaves and bright-red berries. For a good crop, plant both male and female varieties. Ideal specimen or boundary tree or in a shrub border in light shade. Good varieties: 'Golden King' (female, yellow-edged grey-green leaves: shown above); 'Lawsoniana' (female, gold-splashed leaves)

Ilex aquifolium Holly
○ ◐ ◖ ↕ ❖ YEAR-ROUND
H 25m (83ft) S 8m (26ft)

This familiar shrub is slow-growing but will eventually form a good-sized tree. Grown for its glossy, dark, spiny leaves and red berries. To guarantee a good crop, plant both male and female varieties. Good specimen or boundary tree in light shade. Good varieties: 'Argentea Marginata' (female, silver-edged leaves); 'Ferox Argentea' (male, spine-covered, creamy-edged leaves: shown above)

Kalmia angustifolia f. rubra
Sheep laurel

◐💧 pH↓ 🍂 ❖LATE SPRING TO EARLY SUMMER
H 60cm (2ft) S 1.5m (5ft)

Dark rosy-red, bowl-shaped flowers are borne on this mounded shrub with dark-green leaves. It's an ideal understorey plant for the dappled shade under deciduous trees.

Kalmia latifolia Calico bush

◐💧 pH↓ 🍂 ❖LATE SPRING TO MIDSUMMER
H and S 3m (10ft)

The shining, bowl-shaped, pale-pink or white flowers open from dark-pink buds and glow against a backdrop of glossy, dark-green foliage. Good varieties: 'Ostbo Red' (deep-pink flowers open from deep-red buds)

Leucothoe fontanesiana
Switch ivy

◑●💧 pH↓ 🍂 ❖YEAR-ROUND
H 2m (6ft) S 3m (10ft)

This is an upright, bushy shrub with slender leaves on arching stems that carry clusters of white, urn-shaped flowers from early to mid-spring. Perfect for shade anywhere in the garden, even between buildings. Good varieties: 'Rainbow' (dappled cream and pink); L. 'Scarletta' (red-purple emerging leaves)

Mahonia japonica
Japanese barberry

◑●💧 ‖‖ 🍂 ❖LATE AUTUMN TO EARLY SPRING
H 2m (6ft) S 3m (10ft)

A superb architectural evergreen characterized by its ruffs of dark-green, holly-like leaves on upright woody stems and slender spikes of pale-yellow flowers scented like lily-of-the-valley. This is a useful understorey plant for a woodland edge or shrub border in light shade. Good varieties: Bealei Group

Osmanthus × burkwoodii

○◑💧 ‖‖ 🍂 ❖SPRING
H and S 3m (10ft)

A deservedly popular shrub, prized for its delightfully fragrant, jasmine-like white flowers. Lustrous, finely toothed dark-green leaves give it a border presence at other times. This makes a perfect structural addition to a shrubbery or mixed border in light shade, and is a good choice for an eastern-inspired garden design.

Osmanthus delavayi

○◑💧 ‖‖ 🍂 ❖SPRING
H 3m (10ft) S 2m (6ft)

Arching branches bear marvellously fragrant, white jasmine-like flowers throughout mid- to late spring on this domed, evergreen shrub. The handsome, jagged-edged, lustrous, dark grey-green leaves are a fine foil for nearby flowers at other times. Good for a shrubbery or mixed border in light shade, or plant next to a well-used path or entrance to appreciate the fragrance.

Osmanthus heterophyllus
○ ◐ ❄ ▲ ‖ 🍂 ❖YEAR-ROUND
H and S 5m (16ft)

This neat, dome-shaped shrub is worth growing for its lustrous, holly-like leaves alone. Lovely jasmine-scented tubular flowers appear from midsummer to early autumn, followed by blue-black fruit. It makes a fine structural addition to mixed border in light shade. Good varieties: 'Goshiki' (leaves emerge creamy-gold and pink, hardier than species: shown above); 'Purpureus' (leaves emerge blackish purple)

Pachysandra terminalis
Japanese spurge
○– ● ▲ ‖ ❖YEAR-ROUND
H 20cm (8in) S 1m (40in)

A useful. shade-loving, compact evergreen perennial with glossy, toothed leaves and tiny snow-white flowers from late spring to early summer. Perfect for carpeting moist areas between deciduous shrubs and trees, as well as difficult areas of deep shade (under evergreens, between buildings) – provided the soil isn't too dry.

Photinia × fraseri 'Red Robin'
○ ◐ ❄ ▲ ‖ pH→ –pH↑ ❖SPRING
H and S 5m (16ft)

Stunning red, glossy young foliage is the seasonal highlight of this robust hedging shrub that can also be used as a filler plant in a large border. It tolerates shade, but here rarely produces its large, rounded heads of tiny ivory flowers (mid- to late spring), and leaf coloration is less pronounced. Photinia can be clipped as a formal hedge or left to grow informally.

Pieris japonica
Lily-of-the-valley shrub
◐ ▲ pH↓ 🍂 ❖SPRING
H 4m (13ft) S 3m (10ft)

Clusters of pendent white flowers stand out against the glossy foliage of this compact shrub from mid- to late spring. This is a good choice for light shade. Good varieties: 'Flaming Silver' (bright-red emerging foliage, silvery-white edges); 'White Rim' (creamy-yellow edged leaves with pinkish young growth: shown above)

Pittosporum tenuifolium Kohuhu
○ ◐ ❄ ▲ ‖ 🍃 ❖YEAR-ROUND
H 6m (20ft) S 5m (16ft)

Hardy, but only just, this bushy, dome-shaped shrub is clothed in pale-green leaves with wavy edges on black stems. It's ideal for a partially shaded mixed or shrub border that's protected from cold, drying winds. Good varieties: 'Abbotsbury Gold' (green-edged, yellow leaves); 'Irene Paterson' (creamy leaves: shown above); 'Purpureum' (bronze-purple leaves)

Prunus laurocerasus Cherry laurel
○– ● ▲ 🍃 ❖YEAR-ROUND
H 8m (26ft) S 1m (40in)

Dense, bushy shrub with large glossy leaves. It can be grown as a hedge in all types of shade. Spikes of tiny, fragrant white flowers appear in mid-spring, followed by cherry-red fruits that ripen to black. Good varieties: 'Otto Luyken' (compact, with narrow leaves: shown above); 'Rotundifolia' (rounded leaves)

Prunus lusitanica Portugal laurel
○–●◐◖ 🍃 ❖YEAR-ROUND
H 20m (64ft) S 20m (64ft)

Excellent hedging shrub for shady boundaries, where its dense, bushy habit makes an impenetrable barrier. Spikes of tiny, fragrant white flowers are produced in mid-spring, followed by small purple fruits. Tolerates chalky soil and can be trimmed as topiary.

Rhododendron 'Cilpinense'
◐◖ pH↓ ‖‖🍂 ❖EARLY SPRING
H and S 1m (40in)

Delightful, lightly scented whitish-pink, funnel-shaped flowers are produced in abundance during early spring. In milder areas, this rounded bush with its glossy leaves is an ideal choice for a border in light shade in sheltered parts of the garden. Avoid planting this variety where there are frost pockets, because the beautiful flowers are vulnerable to damage.

Rhododendron 'Gumpo White'
Evergreen azalea
◐❄◖ pH↓ ‖‖🍂 ❖EARLY SUMMER
H and S 1m (40in)

Ethereal, funnel-shaped, wavy-edged, white flowers appear during early summer on this lovely dwarf azalea. An ideal choice for a large container on a partially shaded patio. This is not suitable for northerly gardens and requires a sheltered spot.

Rhododendron 'Blue Danube'
Evergreen azalea
◐◖ pH↓ 🍂 ❖LATE SPRING TO EARLY SUMMER
H and S 1m (40in)

This neat, evergreen azalea produces unusual, bluish-mauve, funnel-shaped flowers en masse during late spring and early summer. It is a very hardy variety, able to cope with frost pockets and colder regions of the country as the late-flowering blooms are rarely damaged by frost. Good for light shade almost anywhere in the garden.

Rhododendron 'Doc'
◐◖ pH↓ ‖‖🍂 ❖MID-TO LATE SPRING
H and S 1.2m (4ft)

Round trusses of frilly-edged, funnel-shaped, rosy-pink flowers with darker spots are borne during mid- to late spring and gracefully age to white above contrasting glossy, deep-green, medium-sized leaves. This will light up a partially shaded, sheltered border or can be grown in a large container or raised bed filled with ericaceous compost, but keep out of strong sunshine.

Rhododendron 'Praecox'
H and S 1.5m (5ft)
○◐◖ 🍃 pH↓ ‖‖ ❖LATE WINTER TO EARLY SPRING

A lovely early-flowering, floriferous evergreen rhododendron that produces fabulous displays of purplish-pink, funnel-shaped flowers in trusses during late winter and early spring. This can be grown as an informal flowering hedge in light shade or full sun, or prune it annually after flowering to maintain a neater outline. Buds will open well if cut for indoor decoration.

Sarcococca confusa Christmas box
◐●◖♦🍂❖ EARLY WINTER TO EARLY SPRING
H 1.5m (5ft) S 1m (40in)

The glossy, dark-green foliage of this dense shrub is the perfect foil for the deliciously scented, snow-white flowers that last from early winter to early spring. Rounded, glossy black fruits follow. It's particularly useful in really tough areas of deep shade, such as on the north side of evergreen hedges and between buildings.

Skimmia × confusa 'Kew Green'
◐●◖♦⬍⬍❖ MID- TO LATE SPRING
H 2m (6ft) S 1.5m (5ft)

This is an unusual, green-budded skimmia that forms a neat, dome-shaped shrub. It reveals dense clusters of fragrant, creamy-white flowers during mid- to late spring. Subtle and underrated, this is not the most colourful variety, but it is ideal for shade as it accentuates cool colour schemes, as well as being useful for adding light to shady borders.

Viburnum davidii Viburnum
○◐●◖♦⬍⬍❖ YEAR-ROUND
H and S 1.5m (5ft)

Stunning, metallic-turquoise, bead-like fruits on coral-red stalks are the highlight of this desirable viburnum. They follow the late-spring, flattened heads of white flowers. At other times, the handsome, distinctively veined, dark-green leaves are a fine foil for other plants. This is an excellent border filler and winter-interest shrub for lightly shaded borders.

Sarcococca hookeriana var. *digyna* Christmas box
◐●◖♦⬍⬍❖ EARLY WINTER TO EARLY SPRING
H 1.5m (5ft) S 2m (6ft)

Fragile-looking, white, pink-tinted tassel-like flowers hang in clusters (early winter to early spring) and shine out against the bottle-green foliage of this compact, multi-stemmed shrub. Rounded, glossy black fruits follow. It provides winter interest in a shrubbery or mixed border, or plant next to a well-used shady path or entrance to relish the vanilla fragrance.

Skimmia japonica
Japanese skimmia
◐●◖♦🍂❖ WINTER TO SPRING
H and S 6m (20ft)

An evergreen shrub with slightly aromatic, dark-green leaves and dense clusters of fragrant white or red-tinted mid- to late-spring flowers. On female plants these are followed by stunning red fruits that last most of the winter. It is an excellent container plant. Good varieties: 'Rubella' (male, dark-red flower buds, opening pink: shown above); 'Nymans' (female, white flowers)

Viburnum tinus Laurustinus
○◐●◖♦🍂❖ YEAR-ROUND
H and S 3m(10ft)

A stalwart of the shady border, this useful, conical shrub bears flattened heads of white flowers from early winter to mid-spring, followed by dark blue-black fruit. This is a useful border filler and winter-interest shrub for lightly shaded borders, providing an excellent foil for other plants at other times. Good varieties: 'Gwenllian' (dark pink-budded, pinkish-white flowers: shown above)

Deciduous shrubs

This varied group contains varieties to suit every size of garden and soil type in all degrees of shade. There are low-growing shrubs to cover the ground, or compact forms for front beds, borders and planting up containers. Larger shrubs are ideal for filling gaps and providing structure to the border display, as well as being a summer-long backdrop to other flowering plants.

Year-round value

You can find shrubs to flower in every month of the year, so there's no excuse for long periods without colour and interest, even in a shady garden. Some shrubs have more than one season of note. For example, the variegated dogwood *Cornus alba* 'Elegantissima' (summer leaves and winter stems) or the guelder rose *Viburnum opulus* 'Compactum' (summer flowers with autumn colour and berries). Then there are those that flower for months on end, such as the hardy *Fuchsia* 'Riccartonii' (early summer to mid-autumn), or the flowering quince *Chaenomeles speciosa* 'Moerloosei' (spring).

Shrubs with colourful or notably attractive foliage often have the edge over plain-leaved forms in this respect. Many deciduous varieties offer fantastic bonfire tints during the autumn and a few have such colourful stems or berries that this is their main ornamental appeal.

Take care when planting shrubs not to set them too close together, and once they are established prune them to enhance the full potential of their decorative features (*see* page 53).

The contrasting foliage of an acer and a philadelphus provide impact in a summer flower border.

Deciduous shrubs for acid soil

Acer palmatum
(Japanese maple)

Acer palmatum var. *dissectum*
(cut-leaf Japanese maple)

Enkianthus campanulatus

Hamamelis x *intermedia*
(witch hazel)

See also Deciduous azaleas, right.

Bush roses for shade

Although most roses need full sun for much of the day to flower well, a few can cope with partial shade and still put on a decent display. Here are a few favourites:

'Cardinal de Richelieu' – double, deep burgundy-purple flowers

'Charles de Mills' – double, fragrant, crimson-purple flowers

'Queen of Denmark' – double, fragrant, light-pink flowers

'Roseraie de l'Haÿ' – double, fragrant, magenta flowers

'Tuscany Superb' – double, fragrant, deep crimson-maroon flowers

Deciduous azaleas

If you have an acid soil, and a little extra space to fill, then deciduous azaleas could be the answer. They are hardy and flower as prolifically as evergreen rhododendrons and azaleas (*see* page 87), but have the bonus of fabulous autumn colour. *Rhododendron luteum* is the main species, but there are several garden-worthy hybrids. Many have sweetly scented, colourful, funnel-shaped flowers in late spring and early summer, with nondescript foliage until it takes on vivid shades in autumn. *R. luteum* has yellow flowers and is pretty vigorous, reaching 4 x 4m (13 x 13ft), but the best of the hybrids are more compact. Good hybrids: 'Gibraltar' (orange flowers); 'Homebush' (semi-double, bright-pink flowers); 'Klondyke' (orange flowers); 'Persil' (white flowers)

Acer palmatum Japanese maple
◐💧pH↓ ✿AUTUMN
H and S 5m (16ft)

This deciduous, mound-forming shrub has attractive, palmate foliage that turns brilliant colours in autumn. It looks lovely under deciduous trees, or can be grown in larger containers, but make sure it has a sheltered site to avoid leaf scorch. Good varieties: 'Atropurpureum' (purple leaves, turning red); 'Sango-kaku' (orange-edged leaves, turning yellow)

Acer palmatum var. dissectum
Cut-leaf Japanese maple
◐💧pH↓ ✿AUTUMN
H 2m (6ft) S 3m (10ft)

The shaggy, finely cut foliage of this lovely cut-leaf maple turns wonderful shades in autumn. It forms a compact, mounding shrub or small tree: good in dappled light or in larger containers. Good varieties: 'Garnet' (dark-purple leaves, turning bright red); 'Red Pygmy' (deep-red leaves, turning gold)

Azalea see page 89

Callicarpa bodinieri var. giraldii 'Profusion' Beauty berry
○◐💧⚊pH→-pH↑ ✿YEAR-ROUND
H 3m (10ft) S 2.5m (8ft)

Clusters of stunning, violet bead-like berries remain to decorate the bare branches after the leaves fall in autumn. In addition, this lovely shrub produces small, pink flowers and the young foliage emerges bronze, becoming dark green before an autumn show of pink, red and purple hues. A good-value filler shrub for a partially shaded garden.

Cornus alba 'Elegantissima'
Red-barked dogwood
○◐💧 ✿SUMMER, WINTER
H and S 3m (10ft)

Bright-red stems are revealed when the white-edged, grey-green leaves fall. The flowers are small and creamy-white. Plant in groups next to water in an east- or west-facing border to catch the early-morning or late-evening winter sun. Other good varieties: 'Sibirica' (coral-red stems, dark-green leaves); *C. sanguinea* 'Midwinter Fire' (red-tipped orange-yellow stems)

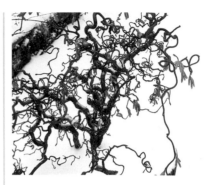

Corylus avellana 'Contorta'
Corkscrew hazel
○◐💧⚊pH→-pH↑ ✿WINTER TO EARLY SPRING
H and S 3m (10ft)

This winter-garden stunner makes a good talking point with its curious-looking, twisted bare stems (much prized by flower arrangers). It bears its drooping, golden-yellow catkins from late winter to early spring before being clothed in puckered hazel leaves in summer.

Enkianthus campanulatus
○◐💧pH↓ ✿LATE SPRING, AUTUMN
H 4m (12ft) S 1.5m (5ft)

This is a double-interest shrub that bears wonderful bell-shaped, pink-tipped creamy flowers, then saves the best until autumn when its oval leaves turn red, orange and yellow. It makes a perfect understorey for a woodland edge or border in dappled shade where it catches the morning or evening sun, though it gives its most brilliant autumn display on acid soil.

Forsythia × intermedia 'Lynwood Variety'
○ ◐ ◑ ◌ ↓↓ ❖ LATE WINTER TO MID-SPRING
H and S 3m (10ft)

Forsythia brings early cheer to the garden when its bare branches are smothered in brilliant yellow flowers. It's a bit nondescript at other times, although the bright-green leaves make a good foil for other flowering plants. Place at the back of a border or grow it as an informal hedge. Other good varieties: F. 'Beatrix Farrand' (orange-yellow flowers, purplish autumn leaves)

Hamamelis × intermedia
Witch hazel
○ ◐ ◑ ◌ pH↓ 🍂 ❖ YEAR-ROUND
H and S 4m (13ft)

Pale-green foliage lifts shade in summer, and yellow and orange foliage tints appear in autumn. Scented, spidery flowers on bare stems stand out against the evergreen foliage of other acid-loving shrubs. Good varieties: 'Arnold Promise' (yellow flowers); 'Diane' (red flowers); 'Jelena' (coppery-red flowers: shown above)

Hydrangea quercifolia 'Snow Queen' Oak-leaved hydrangea
○ ◐ ◑ ◌ ↓↓ 🍂 ❖ LATE SUMMER TO EARLY AUTUMN
H and S 2m (6ft)

This lovely hydrangea offers fabulous value with very attractive oak-leaf-shaped, bright-green foliage that turns pink and red. But it's in late summer and early autumn that it looks its best, when cone-shaped white flower spikes are borne on arching stems. Ideal in a mixed border with moist soil. Other good varieties: 'Snowflake' (shown above)

Fuchsia 'Riccartonii' Hardy fuchsia
○ ◐ ◑ ❄ ◌ ↓↓ ❖ EARLY SUMMER TO MID-AUTUMN
H 2m (6ft) S 3m (10ft)

Scarlet and purple flowers dangle elegantly from arching branches against bronze-tinted foliage. A good front-of-border shrub in partial shade that's protected from cold winds (it's only just hardy), or use as an informal hedge. Other good varieties: 'Mrs Popple' (scarlet and purple-violet flowers); 'Snowcap' (red and white flowers)

Hydrangea arborescens 'Annabelle' Sevenbark
○ ◐ ◌ ◌ ↓↓ 🍂 ❖ MIDSUMMER TO EARLY AUTUMN
H and S 2.5m (8ft)

A brilliant shrub for dappled shade, where its balls of tightly packed, creamy-white flowers shine out from the low light during late summer. The flowerheads fade gracefully as they mature and the two-tone leaves turn yellow. Other good varieties: 'Vanille Fraise' (compact, with creamy-white flowers that age to pink, then red)

Kerria japonica Jew's mallow
○ ◐ ◑ ◌ ◌ ↓↓ ❖ EARLY TO MID-SPRING
H 2m (6ft) S 2.5m (8ft)

Golden, buttercup-like flowers are produced on stiffly arching stems with emerging toothed, fresh-green foliage. Easy shrub for a partially shaded border. Good varieties: 'Golden Guinea' (large flowers); 'Picta' (orange-yellow flowers, white-variegated leaves); 'Pleniflora' (double yellow flowers: shown above)

Lonicera × purpusii 'Winter Beauty' Winter honeysuckle

○ ◑ ◐ ○ ⇊ ❖ EARLY WINTER TO EARLY SPRING

H 2m (6ft) S 2.5m (8ft)

This is a joy of the winter garden when its clusters of white, tubular flowers with prominent yellow anthers decorate bare branches. A rounded shrub with purple-stained shoots and dark-green leaves, it is ideal for a mixed border, or plant it next to a path to appreciate the fragrance.

Magnolia stellata Star magnolia

○ ◑ ◐ ○ ⇊ ❖ SPRING

H 3m (10ft) S 4m (13ft)

This is a wonderful, compact, bushy magnolia. It becomes smothered with masses of silky buds, which open to reveal dainty snow-white or pink-flushed white, scented, star-shaped flowers on bare stems in early spring. An excellent specimen for partially shaded areas and a particularly good choice where space is limited. Good varieties: 'Royal Star' (white flowers)

Paeonia delavayi var. *delavayi* Tree peony

○ ◑ ◐ ⇊ ❖ MID-SPRING TO EARLY SUMMER

H 2m (6ft) S 1.2m (4ft)

Sumptuous, maroon-red, cup-shaped flowers up to 10cm (4in) across are carried over a mound of burgundy-flushed foliage that matures to dark green. Plant in a mixed border in partial shade next to a path so that you can appreciate these stunning blooms.

Philadelphus coronarius Mock orange

○ ◑ ◐ ○ ⇊ ❖ EARLY TO MIDSUMMER

H 2.4m (8ft) S 1.8m (6ft)

Well known for their heady summer fragrance, philadelphus are justifiably popular, with varieties to suit every garden. Plant it in a sheltered spot to allow the lovely orange-blossom aroma to drift on the air on warm summer's evenings. Ideal for a mixed border in partial shade, especially next to seating areas. Other good varieties: 'Virginal' (double white flowers)

Prunus triloba Flowering almond

○ ◑ ◐ ○ ⇊ ❖ LATE SPRING

H and S 3m (10ft)

This lovely flowering almond bears bowl-shaped, peach-pink flowers. The rounded, finely toothed fresh-green leaves take on attractive yellow and bronze tints in autumn. Ideal for a small, shady garden.

Rubus cockburnianus White-stemmed bramble

○–● ◐ ○ ⇊ ❖ WINTER

H and S 2.5m (8ft)

The stiff, prickly, purple stems of this thicket-forming shrub have a ghostly white bloom, which is a highlight of the winter garden. Plant it where it is back-lit by low winter sun for an eerie effect. The two-tone ferny foliage is attractive all summer too. Note that it can be invasive in confined spaces, though.

Sambucus racemosa 'Sutherland Gold' Red-berried elder

○ ◑ ◔ ♦ ♯ ❖ SPRING TO AUTUMN
H and S 3m (10ft)

Stunning, finely cut foliage on arching stems emerges bronze before turning a glorious golden colour. As a bonus, creamy mid-spring flowers are followed by glossy red fruits. Best in partial shade since foliage can scorch in full sun. Other good varieties: *S. nigra* 'Eva' (pink flowers, deep-purple foliage)

Symphoricarpos × doorenbosii 'White Hedge' Snowberry

○ ◑ ◔ ♯ ❖ MIDSUMMER TO AUTUMN
H 1.5m (5ft) S 1m (40in)

Curious, long-lasting clusters of white fruits following inconspicuous flowers are the main point of interest here. A rather nondescript shrub for much of the year, forming a spreading thicket of stems and foliage. Suitable for a woodland edge or in a partially shaded wild area of the garden though. Other good varieties: 'Mother of Pearl'

Viburnum × bodnantense 'Charles Lamont'

○ ◑ ◔ ◌ ♯ ❖ LATE AUTUMN TO EARLY SPRING
H 3m (10ft) S 2m (6ft)

The heavenly-scented, bright-pink flowers borne on bare stems are a delight. Oblong, toothed, dark-green foliage is a useful foil for other plants during the summer months. This gives good winter interest in a mixed border in partial shade – plant next to a path to appreciate the fragrance. Other good varieties: 'Dawn' (rosy-pink flowers)

Viburnum opulus 'Compactum' Guelder rose

○ ◑ ◔ ♯ ❖ EARLY SUMMER, AUTUMN
H and S 1.5m (5ft)

Stunning, fiery shades in autumn are the main feature of this compact viburnum, although the white lacecap flowers and bright-red autumn fruits are attractive too. Ideal for a wildlife area or a woodland edge. Other good varieties: 'Roseum' (white ball-shaped flowerheads)

Viburnum plicatum f. tomentosum 'Mariesii' Japanese snowball bush

○ ◑ ◔ ♯ ❖ LATE SPRING, AUTUMN
H 3m (10ft) S 4m (13ft)

This beautiful, horizontally tiered shrub bears white lacecap flowers that age gracefully to pink. The toothed, distinctly veined foliage is attractive in autumn when it turns purple. Other good varieties: 'Pink Beauty' (white flowers, turning pink); 'Summer Snowflake' (more compact, longer flowering: late spring to early autumn)

Weigela 'Florida Variegata'

○ ◑ ◔ ♯ ❖ EARLY SUMMER
H and S 2.5m (8ft)

A pretty, variegated shrub with white-edged, grey-green leaves on gracefully arching stems that offer double the value in early summer when they become smothered in funnel-shaped, pale-pink flowers. Other good varieties: 'Bristol Ruby' (dark-red flowers)

Climbers and wall shrubs

Climbers and wall shrubs are very much a bonus in the garden because they offer so much and take so little space. As well as being an attractive feature in their own right, climbers can be used in many other ways in the shady garden: covering ugly walls and fences, adding height to borders, defining focal points and features, or serving as an unusual ground cover. Many climbers can be grown in containers, too.

Morello cherry will grow well against a shady wall, even a north-facing one, though it likes well-drained soil.

Size and hardiness

Before choosing a climber consider both its ultimate size for the space available and its hardiness. Although most climbers can be kept under control by pruning, this is not only time-consuming, but may adversely affect their flowering performance. Some climbers are only borderline hardy, especially in an exposed position, so make sure you get one man enough for the location.

Note that a few varieties don't like wet feet in winter and one or two do best in acid soil.

Of course, in a shady garden, the climber should be able to tolerate the shadows for at least part of the day. In a south-facing garden, you can grow sun-loving climbers to provide much-needed shade (*see* page 21).

Clematis

For colour and interest all year round, choose climbers with complementary flowering times, such as clematis. Through early and late spring *Clematis armandii*, *C. alpina* and *C. macropetala* varieties are in full bloom. By early summer varieties of *C. montana* and the early-flowering hybrids reach their peak, followed by the later-flowering hybrid clematis and varieties of *C. tangutica*. Autumn sees many a second flush from early-flowering hybrids, which can be enhanced by relay pruning (*see* page 54), followed by winter-flowering *C. cirrhosa* varieties.

Clematis hybrids

There is a huge range of colourful varieties to choose from. These are some favourites (*see* page 54 for information about pruning groups). All are hardy.

'Alba Luxurians' – purple-centred white flowers (midsummer to early autumn), pruning group 3.

'Arctic Queen' – creamy-centred double white flowers (late spring to early summer and late summer to early autumn), pruning group 2.

'Bees' Jubilee' – deep-pink flowers with darker stripe (late spring to early summer and early autumn), pruning group 2.

'Belle of Woking' – creamy-centred **double** silvery-lilac flowers (late spring to early summer and early autumn), pruning group 2.

'Betty Corning' – mauve-edged, creamy-white flowers (midsummer to mid-autumn), pruning group 3.

'Bill MacKenzie' – yellow, bell-shaped flowers (midsummer to early autumn), pruning group 3.

'Comtesse de Bouchaud' – yellow-centred mauve-pink flowers (midsummer to early autumn), pruning group 3.

'Duchess of Albany' – deep-pink flowers, with lighter stripe (midsummer to mid-autumn), pruning group 3.

'Ernest Markham' – creamy-centred red flowers (midsummer to mid-autumn), pruning group 3.

'Etoile Violette' – creamy-centred, deep-purple flowers (midsummer to early autumn), pruning group 3.

'Gravetye Beauty' – crimson flowers (midsummer to mid-autumn), pruning group 3.

'Jackmanii Superba' – velvety purple flowers (mid- to late summer), pruning group 3.

'Lasurstern' – creamy-centred mid-blue flowers (late spring to early summer and early autumn), pruning group 2.

'Nelly Moser' – pale-pink striped, pink flowers (late spring to early summer and early autumn), pruning group 2.

'Niobe' – rich deep-red flowers (midsummer to early autumn), pruning group 2.

'The President' – red-centred purple-blue flowers (early summer to early autumn), pruning group 2.

'Ville de Lyon' – yellow-centred carmine-red flowers (midsummer to early autumn), pruning group 3.

'Vyvyan Pennell' – yellow-centred, double, violet and purple flowers (late spring to early summer and early autumn), pruning group 2.

Akebia quinata Chocolate vine
○ ◐ 🌢 ‖ ❖SPRING
H 10m (32ft) S 2m (6ft)

This dainty climber, once established, bears clusters of spicy, chocolate-scented, wine-red flowers. The backdrop of bright-green foliage becomes purple-flushed in colder weather. If the summer is long and warm, you will also get a crop of unusual, sausage-shaped seedpods. Grow this to cover a partially shaded arch so that the fragrant flowers can be seen from below.

Chaenomeles speciosa
Flowering quince
○ ◐ 🌢 ‖ ❖EARLY TO LATE SPRING
H 2.5m (8ft) S 5m (16ft)

A vigorous wall shrub with striking scarlet flowers. It needs to be pruned to form an upright shape. Invaluable for adding a splash of colour to east- and west-facing boundaries. Good varieties (both smaller than C. speciosa): 'Geisha Girl' (apricot-pink flowers); 'Nivalis' (white flowers)

Clematis alpina
○ ◐ 🌢 ◌ ‖ ❖MID- TO LATE SPRING
H 3m (10ft) S 1.5m (5ft)

Delightful early-flowering climber carrying tiny, nodding, bell-shaped blue flowers with creamy centres. Fluffy seedheads follow. Pruning group 1. Good varieties: C. 'Frankie' (larger, light-blue flowers); C. 'Helsingsborg' (bluish-purple flowers); C. 'Pink Flamingo' (deep-pink flowers); C. 'Ruby' (shown above)

Clematis armandii
○ ◐ ❄ 🌢 ◌ ‖ ❖EARLY TO MID-SPRING
H 5m (16ft) S 3m (10ft)

The gorgeous, star-shaped, creamy flowers (with a lovely almond scent) of this popular clematis stand out against a backdrop of glossy, evergreen leaves. Although frost hardy, it needs shelter from cold winds. Pruning group 1. Good varieties: 'Apple Blossom' (pink-flushed white flowers)

Clematis cirrhosa var. balearica
○ ◐ ❄ 🌢 ◌ ‖ ❖WINTER
H 3m (10ft) S 1.5m (5ft)

You need to get close to this bronze-tinted, evergreen clematis to fully appreciate the reddish-maroon freckling inside the fragrant, creamy-white flowers. Although frost hardy, it needs shelter from cold winds. Pruning group 1. Good varieties: var. purpurascens 'Freckles' (creamy flowers, speckled with red); 'Wisley Cream' (small creamy flowers)

Clematis macropetala
○ ◐ 🌢 ◌ ‖ ❖MID- TO LATE SPRING, SUMMER
H 3m (10ft) S 1.5m (5ft)

Beautiful bell-shaped, violet-blue flowers with creamy centres decorate this deciduous clematis. Attractive silky seedheads follow and provide interest throughout the summer. Pruning group 1. Good varieties: C. 'Floral Feast' (shown above); C. 'Jan Lindmark' (mauve flowers); 'Lagoon' (deep-blue flowers)

Clematis montana
○ ◐ ♦ ◊ ↕ ❖ LATE SPRING TO EARLY SUMMER
H 12m (40ft) S 3m (10ft)

This vigorous, dark-green clematis is smothered in small white flowers with creamy-yellow centres. It's ideal for covering shady eyesores and stark vertical surfaces. Pruning group 1. Good varieties: *C. 'Elizabeth'* (fragrant, yellow-centred soft-pink flowers); *C. 'Marjorie'* (semi-double pink-centred creamy-pink flowers); var. *rubens* 'Tetrarose' (fragrant yellow-centred deep-pink flowers)

Clematis tangutica
○ ◐ ♦ ◊ ↕ ❖ MIDSUMMER TO WINTER
H 6m (20ft) S 3m (10ft)

The cheerful yellow lanterns of this vigorous clematis brighten up partially shaded walls and fences. Deliciously fluffy seedheads follow the flowers. This is also a good choice for covering pergolas and arches, or west- or east-facing walls and fences. Pruning group 3.

Celastrus orbiculatus
Oriental bittersweet
○ ◐ ♦ ◊ ↕ ❖ AUTUMN
H 12m (40ft) S 4m (13ft)

A vigorous, deciduous climber with rounded, scalloped, mid-green leaves that turn butter yellow in autumn. At this time, yellow seed capsules split to reveal glistening pink and scarlet fruits.

Cotoneaster horizontalis
○ ◐ ♦ ◊ ↕ ❖ LATE SPRING, AUTUMN
H 2m (6ft) S 3m (10ft)

This reliable wall shrub produces an attractive herringbone pattern of branches against a shady wall. It is encrusted with tiny, pinkish-white flowers in late spring, followed by scarlet autumn berries beloved of birds. The tiny, glossy, dark-green leaves look neat all summer and turn red before falling. This is a superb choice for a north-facing wall, or it can be used as a deep, woody ground cover in partially shaded areas.

Fallopia baldschuanica
Russian vine
○ ◐ ♦ ◊ ↕ ❖ LATE SUMMER TO EARLY AUTUMN
H 12m (40ft) S 4m (13ft)

This brute of a deciduous climber will cover large outbuildings or garden structures in a few seasons, but use with care, since it can be overwhelming. In a sunny garden it provides useful shade. It is smothered with sprays of tiny, funnel-shaped, pink-flushed white flowers.

Garrya elliptica Silk-tassel bush
○ ◐ ❄ ♦ ◊ ↕ ❖ WINTER
H and S 4m (13ft)

An easy-to-grow evergreen wall shrub that bears slender grey-green catkins up to 15cm (6in) long, which provide winter interest. The wavy-edged, glossy dark-green leaves offer a decorative cover at other times and are an excellent foil for other plants throughout the year. It looks best trained against a shady east- or west-facing wall, or a fence that provides a little shelter. Good varieties: 'James Roof'; *G.* x *issaquahensis* 'Glasnevin Wine' (purple-stained catkins)

Hedera algeriensis
Canary Island ivy

○ ◐ ❄ ♦ ◊ pH→ –pH↑ ↓↓ ❖ YEAR-ROUND
H 4m (13ft) S 5m (16ft)

Huge, shining, silvery evergreen leaves on dark-red stalks provide a cloak of foliage over vertical surfaces. Perfect for brightening up partially shaded corners (but needs shelter from cold winds) and good in containers on a sheltered patio. Good varieties: 'Gloire de Marengo' (creamy-edged leaves: shown above)

Hedera colchica Persian ivy

○–● ♦ ◊ pH→ –pH↑ ❖ YEAR-ROUND
H 10m (32ft) S 5m (16ft)

This is another handsome, vigorous, self-clinging climber that soon covers vertical surfaces. Its evergreen leaves are large, shiny and heart-shaped. Variegated forms brighten up gloomy areas where little else will grow. Good varieties: 'Dentata Variegata' (creamy-edged grey-green leaves); 'Sulphur Heart' (creamy-yellow splodged, bright-green leaves: shown above)

Hedera hibernica Irish ivy

○ ◐ ♦ ◊ ↓↓ pH→ –pH↑ ❖ YEAR-ROUND
H 1m (40in) S 1.2m (4ft)

Lovely ivy with five-lobed, arrow-shaped dark-green leaves. Once mature (can be slow to establish), this self-clinging evergreen produces sprays of yellowish-green flowers from mid- to late autumn, followed by black fruits. Any soil will do, but it prefers alkaline: in containers use John Innes No.3 potting compost. Good cover for low walls and fences, and useful for softening shady paving edges.

Hydrangea anomala subsp. petiolaris Climbing hydrangea

○–● ♦ ◊ ↓↓ ❖ LATE SPRING TO AUTUMN
H 15m (48ft) S 3m (10ft)

Lift cold, shady walls with this self-clinging deciduous climber. The creamy-white lacecap flowers in late spring and early summer stand out against the dark-green leaves, which turn butter yellow in autumn. It's slow to get going, but will grow 50cm (20in) a year once established.

Jasminum nudiflorum
Winter jasmine

○ ◐ ♦ ◊ ↓↓ ❖ EARLY WINTER TO EARLY SPRING
H and S 3m (10ft)

This is a real star of the winter garden, offering lemon-yellow flowers. The stiff, bright-green bare stems can be left to scramble informally over low walls, or tie them into trellis or horizontal wires.

Parthenocissus henryana
Chinese Virginia creeper

◐ ❄ ♦ ◊ ↓↓ ❖ SUMMER TO AUTUMN
H 10m (32ft) S 5m (16ft)

A beautiful deciduous climber with dark-green, velvety, five-lobed leaves decorated with white and pink veins. It turns fiery shades of scarlet in autumn. An ideal choice for covering north-, east- or west-facing walls and fences that do not get too cold in winter. Being less vigorous than some of its relations, this is ideal for smaller gardens.

Parthenocissus quinquefolia
Virginia creeper
○–●●◊ ‼ ❖AUTUMN
H 15m (50ft) S 5m (16ft)

This is arguably the best ornamental creeper for autumn colour, and it's vigorous and fast-growing. The deeply divided leaves ignite into dramatic fiery shades of crimson before they fall.

Pyracantha Firethorn
○●●◊ ‼ ❖AUTUMN TO WINTER
H 3m (10ft) S 4m (13ft)

This superb evergreen is mainly grown for its abundant clusters of bead-like autumn and winter berries beloved of native songbirds. The upright, spiny-stemmed shrub also produces small white flowers in late spring. Good for fan-training against a partially shaded east- or west-facing wall or fence, or as an informal flowering hedge. It can be grown free-standing, too. Good varieties: 'Dart's Red' (clear-red berries); 'Mohave' (shown above); 'Orange Glow' (long-lasting orange berries); 'Soleil d'Or' (golden berries)

Rosa 'Albéric Barbier'
○●●◊ ‼🍂 ❖EARLY SUMMER, EARLY AUTUMN
H 5m (16ft) S 4m (13ft)

Virtually evergreen, this vigorous, rambling rose produces uplifting sprays of double, slightly scented, creamy flowers in early summer (often with a repeat performance in early autumn) that stand out against the glossy, dark-green leaves. Use to cover walls, fences and other structures in partial shade.

Rosa 'Madame Alfred Carrière'
○–●●◊ ‼🍂 ❖MIDSUMMER TO EARLY AUTUMN
H 5m (16ft) S 3m (10ft)

An old-fashioned, repeat-flowering climbing rose that bears fragrant, double white or pale-pink flowers into early autumn. The pliable stems are ideal for training so it's a good choice for arches and pergolas in partial shade, as well as east-, west- or north-facing vertical surfaces.

Rosa 'Zéphirine Drouhin'
○–●●‼🍂 ❖SUMMER TO EARLY AUTUMN
H 3m (10ft) S 2m (6ft)

A lovely repeat-flowering Bourbon rose smothered in fragrant, double, deep-pink flowers. Its thornless stems make it ideal for arches and pergolas, and its tolerance of deep shade means it will cover north-facing walls.

Schizophragma hydrangeoides
Japanese hydrangea vine
○●●◊ ‼🍂 ❖EARLY SUMMER
H 12m (40ft) S 3m (10ft)

With cream-coloured flowers like those of the lacecap hydrangeas, this lovely vine is ideal for covering house and garden walls. It's slow to get going, but should eventually grow 50cm (20in) a year.

Ground cover

Ground-hugging plants that smother weeds and carpet the ground with an attractive tapestry of foliage and flowers are a key ingredient in an easy-care, shady garden. Good ground-cover plants not only need to be able to tolerate shade, but should ideally form a dense covering of foliage throughout the year and be attractive in their own right. The best varieties are those that also require little or no maintenance.

Use ground-cover plants next to paths and to fill any shady gaps.

Ways to use ground cover

Ground-cover plants are useful in a number of ways. They are ideal for covering bare soil between established trees and for skirting around shrubs. Choose plants that will complement the existing display, adding interest when the shrub or tree is looking dull.

For example, between deciduous shrubs in winter, try planting a shag-pile carpet of bergenia (elephant's ears) with its attractive winter tints and brightly coloured flowers that appear before the shrubs fully leaf-up in spring.

Solving problem areas

Another way to use ground cover is as an alternative to a conventional lawn in areas of low light, where grasses will struggle to thrive.

It can also be used to cover shady banks that are too difficult to mow. Here, try planting easy-care perennials such as pulmonaria or shade-tolerant, hummock-forming shrubs, like *Euonymus fortunei* 'Emerald 'n' Gold', which will add colour and interest with its yellow-variegated foliage. Euonymus also works well under trees, creating a dense, low-growing understorey.

In areas of deep shade where the soil is dry and little else will grow, it's always worth trying *Euphorbia amygdaloides* var. *robbiae*, *Hypericum* x *moserianum* 'Tricolor' or *Ruscus aculeatus* (butcher's broom).

Narrow strips alongside fences or sheds and garages are other common problem areas that can get neglected. You can prevent these becoming a stronghold for weeds by filling them with robust plants such as variegated ivies and periwinkle.

A few choices for dry shade

Brunnera macrophylla
(Siberian bugloss)

Euphorbia amygdaloides
(wood spurge)

Geranium macrorrhizum
(hardy cranesbill)

Hedera helix
(common ivy)

Hypericum x *moserianum* 'Tricolor'
(St John's wort)

Prunella grandiflora
(self-heal)

Rubus tricolor

Ruscus aculeatus
(butcher's broom)

Saxifraga x *urbium*
(London pride)

Vinca minor
(lesser periwinkle)

Ground cover for acid shade

Asarum europaeum
(wild ginger)

Gaultheria procumbens
(wintergreen)

Ground cover for deep shade

Asarum europaeum
(wild ginger)

Euphorbia amygdaloides
(wood spurge)

Hedera helix
(common ivy)

Hosta
(plantain lily) – some

Hypericum x *moserianum* 'Tricolor'
(St. John's wort)

Ruscus aculeatus
(butcher's broom)

Saxifraga x *urbium*
(London pride)

Tiarella cordifolia
(foam flower)

Ajuga reptans Bugle
○ ◑ ◐ ◌ ‡‡ ❖YEAR-ROUND
H 15cm (6in) S 1m (40in)

A superb semi-evergreen with short spikes of deep-blue flowers that carpets the ground all year unless the weather turns really cold. It likes moisture-retentive ground and can tolerate very poor soils. Good under deciduous shrubs and for edging a partially shaded border. Good varieties: 'Burgundy Glow' (wine-red and cream-splodged foliage); 'Catlin's Giant' (glossy bronze-purple leaves: shown above)

Asarum europaeum Wild ginger
◑ ◐ ◌ pH↓ 🌿 ❖YEAR-ROUND
H 8cm (3in) S 30cm (12in)

Carpets of glossy, deep-green, kidney-shaped leaves make this creeping evergreen perennial perfect as an edging or ground-cover plant for partially shaded areas where the soil does not dry out in summer: it will tolerate deep shade too. As a bonus in early to mid-spring (after a warm summer), hooded purplish-red flowers strive to poke out from the foliage.

Brunnera macrophylla
Siberian bugloss
◑ ◐ ◌ ◌ ❖MID- TO LATE SPRING
H 45cm (18in) S 60cm (2ft)

Pretty, bright-blue forget-me-not-like flowers appear above clumps of large, green, heart-shaped leaves. This is a useful ground cover as it will tolerate dry soil conditions in partial shade once it's established. Good varieties: 'Jack Frost' (leaves marbled with silvery-white: shown above)

Alchemilla mollis Lady's mantle
○ ◑ ◐ ◌ ◌ ❖EARLY SUMMER TO EARLY AUTUMN
H 60cm (2ft) S 75cm (30in)

The frothy haze of lady mantle's tiny yellow flowers are a mainstay of the summer border, in partial shade or full sun. Its scalloped foliage holds water droplets like quicksilver. It will grow in all types of soil, including heavy clay, and it is drought tolerant. Clip off faded flowers to prevent excessive seeding around.

Bergenia Elephant's ears
○ ◑ ◐ ◌ ◌ ‡‡ ❖YEAR-ROUND
H 30cm (12in) S 60cm (2ft)

Tough as old boots, the large, leathery, oval leaves of bergenia make excellent low-maintenance, evergreen ground cover anywhere from partial or dappled shade to full sun. The spring flowers, usually pink or white, are a bonus. It will grow in heavy clay to fairly dry soils. Good varieties: 'Abendglut' (magenta flowers); 'Bressingham White' (white flowers); 'Silberlicht' (white flowers, fading to pink: shown above)

Convallaria majalis
Lily-of-the-valley
○ ◑ ◌ 🌿 ❖MID- TO LATE SPRING
H 25cm (10in) S 30cm (12in)

The classic white hanging bells of this familiar plant quickly spread to form a fragrant carpet in mid- to late spring. Excellent under deciduous trees and shrubs or for lightly shaded areas with humus-rich soil elsewhere in the garden.

Epimedium perralderianum
Barrenwort

◑◒♦🍂 ❖YEAR-ROUND
H 30cm (12in) S 60cm (2ft)

This trusty barrenwort has attractive, heart-shaped evergreen leaves that take on reddish tints later in the year. Airy clouds of tiny, bright-yellow spring flowers are held on delicate stems from mid- to late spring. Good varieties: *E.* x *perralchicum* 'Frohnleiten' (decorative foliage, flushed with bronze in spring)

Epimedium x youngianum
'Niveum' Bishop's mitre

◑♦🍂 ❖YEAR-ROUND
H and S 30cm (12in)

Bishop's mitre carries airy sprays of snow-white flowers above its bronze-tinted, pale-green leaves from mid- to late spring. The leaf stalks are tinted red. This is an excellent choice under deciduous trees or for lightly shaded areas elsewhere in the garden.

Euonymus fortunei
○◑♦◊ ⇅ ❖YEAR-ROUND
H 60cm (2ft) S 1m (40in)

A reliable stalwart with glossy, leathery leaves. Variegated forms are excellent for lifting a partially shaded shrub border or wall. Tiny green flowers from late spring to early summer are followed by spherical white fruits. Good varieties: 'Emerald 'n' Gold' (yellow-edged leaves, becoming pink-tinged in winter: shown above); 'Harlequin' (trailing, leaves speckled yellow, cream and pink)

Euphorbia amygdaloides
Wood spurge

●◑♦◊ ⇅ ❖YEAR-ROUND
H 60cm (2ft) S 30cm (12in)

A bushy evergreen perennial with rosettes of dark-green leaves on reddish stems; tall clusters of lime-green flowers appear from mid-spring into early summer. This is useful in dry, shady areas between buildings or at the bottom of hedges, but it can be invasive. Good varieties: var. *robbiae* (lime-green flowers); 'Purpurea' (acid-yellow flowers, purple-mahogany leaves: shown above)

Gaultheria procumbens
Wintergreen

◑♦ pH↓ 🌿 ❖YEAR-ROUND
H 15cm (6in) S 1m (40in)

In late spring and early summer, white or pale-pink, urn-shaped flowers are set off against a carpet of glossy, dark-green leaves that take on reddish tinges in winter. Aromatic, scarlet fruits follow the flowers. This is good between larger shrubs and trees, or as a permanent edge to acid woodland paths where the foliage will perfume the air when crushed underfoot.

Geranium macrorrhizum
Hardy cranesbill

○◑♦◊ ⇅ ❖MIDSUMMER TO MID-AUTUMN
H 50cm (20in) S 60cm (2ft)

Lovely purple-pink, saucer-shaped flowers are carried above low mounds of aromatic, deeply cut, pale-green leaves. The foliage takes on orange-yellow shades in autumn. This is a good weed-suppressing cover in partial shade, and it copes well in dry shade too. Good varieties: 'Album' (white flowers); 'Bevan's Variety' (crimson-purple flowers); 'Spessart' (pale-pink flowers)

Hedera helix Common ivy

○–●◐○ pH→ –pH↑ 🌿 ❖YEAR-ROUND
H 1m (40in) S 5m (16ft)

Everyone knows this vigorous, self-clinging climber. It's perfect for covering dry, shady areas under shrubs and trees and will quickly smother walls and fences. This ivy prefers alkaline soil, but in fact any kind will do. Good varieties: 'Buttercup' (bright-yellow leaves in sun, pale green in shade: shown above); 'Parsley Crested' (curled-edged leaves); 'Glacier' (grey-green leaves with silver and cream markings)

Hosta sieboldiana Plantain lily

○–●◐♦ ↓↓ ❖LATE SPRING TO LATE SUMMER
H 1m (40in) S 1.2m (4ft)

A lovely clump-forming herbaceous perennial with large, puckered, heart-shaped blue-grey leaves. Dusty lilac, trumpet-shaped flowers appear in midsummer. It forms a deep ground cover in moist, shady areas that are sheltered from cold, drying winds. Good varieties: var. *elegans* (blue leaves: shown above); *H.* 'Frances Williams' (blue-green leaves with greeny-yellow margins)

Lamium maculatum

○◐♦ ↓↓ ❖LATE SPRING TO MIDSUMMER
H 20cm (8in) S 1m (40in)

Low-growing and mat-forming, this perennial has toothed, nettle-shaped leaves, often striped with silvery white, and spikes of white, pink or purple flowers. It's excellent in between shrubs, or in difficult spaces between buildings. Good varieties: 'Beacon Silver' (green-edged silver leaves, pale-pink flowers); 'Pink Pearls' (white-striped leaves, pale-pink flowers); 'Red Nancy' (green-edged silver leaves, purplish-red flowers)

Heuchera Coral flower

○◐♦ ↓↓ ❖YEAR-ROUND
H and S 60cm (2ft)

This fantastic evergreen foliage perennial produces neat mounds of often colourful and boldly veined leaves. Wiry stems carry airy sprays of tiny summer flowers. Suits lightly shaded areas. Good varieties: 'Chocolate Ruffles' (chocolate-brown leaves, white flowers); 'Obsidian' (black-maroon leaves, white flowers); 'Plum Pudding' (silver-dusted, purple foliage, pale-pink flowers: shown above)

Hypericum × moserianum 'Tricolor' St John's wort

○–●◐♦○ ↓↓ ❖MIDSUMMER TO MID-AUTUMN
H 30cm (12in) S 60cm (2ft)

Uplifting butter-yellow, cup-shaped flowers on red stems decorate low-spreading, semi-evergreen mounds of eye-catching cream and pink variegated leaves. This needs protection from cold winter winds but it is good ground cover for difficult, dry, shady areas where little else will grow.

Lysimachia nummularia Creeping Jenny

○◐♦ 🌿 ❖SUMMER
H 5cm (2in) S 50cm (20in)

A fast-growing, carpeting plant with tiny, rounded, dark-green leaves. It is covered in brilliant-yellow flowers throughout summer. Good for moist areas in partial shade and useful for softening the edges of hard land-scaping, but beware, it can be invasive. Good varieties: 'Aurea' (golden-yellow leaves: shown above)

Nepeta x faassenii Catmint
○ ◐ ◑ ◊ ⚌ ❖ EARLY SUMMER TO EARLY AUTUMN
H 45cm (18in) S 45cm (18in)

Vigorous mounds of aromatic, light grey-green hairy leaves provide an attractive foil for the spikes of lavender-blue flowers. This plant is loved by bees and other beneficial insects. Cats like to lie in it too – hence its common name.

Persicaria affinis 'Donald Lowndes'
○ ◐ ◑ ◊ ❖ YEAR-ROUND
H 20cm (8in) S 30cm (12in)

Dense, bottlebrush flower spikes emerge pale pink and age to deep pink between midsummer and mid-autumn above a thick, evergreen carpet of lance-shaped leaves. The bronze-tinted foliage is a feature in winter, too. This provides good year-round cover for moist areas.

Prunella grandiflora Self-heal
○ ◐ ◑ ◊ ◊ ❖ EARLY TO MIDSUMMER
H 15cm (6in) S 1m (40in)

This spreading perennial forms a dense mat of evergreen, spearhead-shaped, dark-green leaves from which spikes of deep violet-purple flowers appear. Self-heal copes well with dry shady areas.

Pulmonaria saccharata
◑ ◊ ⚌ ❖ YEAR-ROUND
H 30cm (12in) S 60cm (2ft)

Clusters of funnel-shaped, reddish-violet to white flowers appear sporadically from late winter to late spring on this clump-forming evergreen. Useful in any partially shaded areas where the white-spotted leaves will lighten the gloom. Good varieties: Argentea Group (reddish-violet flowers); 'Mrs Moon' (bluish-lilac flowers); 'Dora Bielefeld' (pink flowers)

Rubus tricolor
○ ◐ ◑ ◊ ◊ ⚌ ❖ YEAR-ROUND
H 60cm (2ft) S 1m (40in)

A creeping, hairy-stemmed evergreen with glossy, deeply veined dark-green leaves that are silver beneath. The white, saucer-shaped midsummer flowers are followed by red fruits in early autumn. This is good between shrubs or for softening the edges to paths, and it copes well with dry shade too.

Ruscus aculeatus Butcher's broom
○ – ◐ ◑ ◊ ◊ ⚌ ❖ AUTUMN
H 75cm (30in) S 1m (40in)

An unusual, clump-forming evergreen subshrub, with spine-tipped, leaf-like flattened stems, that forms a dense scrub under trees. On female plants, the inconspicuous, early-spring flowers are followed by bead-like red fruits. It's reliable under trees, especially on dry soils where nothing else will grow, but it doesn't like waterlogged conditions.

Saxifraga x *urbium* London pride
○–●◐○↓↓❖LATE SPRING TO EARLY SUMMER
H 30cm (12in) S 15cm (6in)

Delightful frothy clouds of white, pink-centred flowers on wiry stems last until early summer on this carpeting perennial with rosettes of spoon-shaped, crimped leaves. This is a useful plant for lightly shaded areas with poor soil, as long as it doesn't dry out completely.

Symphytum grandiflorum
Comfrey
○◐◐❖MID- TO LATE SPRING
H 40cm (16in) S 60cm (2ft)

Comfrey has pendent clusters of nectar-rich, tubular flowers above mounds of attractive, hairy foliage. It is a fine choice for woodland edges and wildflower areas in dappled shade, but it's invasive. Good varieties: 'Hidcote Blue' (pale-blue flowers); 'Hidcote Pink' (pink and white flowers); 'Goldsmith' (creamy-yellow variegated foliage and light-blue, cream or pink flowers: shown above)

Tellima grandiflora Fringe cups
◐◐❖LATE SPRING TO MIDSUMMER
H 80cm (32in) S 30cm (12in)

Dancing, slender spikes of bell-shaped, white or greenish-white flowers provide an airy contrast to the rosettes of hairy, heart-shaped, emerald-green leaves. This is an excellent semi-evergreen choice for a partially shaded woodland edge, or a shrub border that's sheltered from cold winds.

Tiarella cordifolia Foam flower
◐◐●❖LATE SPRING TO AUTUMN
H and S 30cm (12in)

This semi-evergreen is a useful, spreading shade-lover. Airy spikes of creamy-white, star-shaped flowers froth above a layered carpet of hairy, maple-like, fresh-green leaves that become bronze-tinted in autumn.

Trifolium pratense 'Susan Smith' (syn. 'Gold Net')
○◐◐❖LATE SPRING TO LATE SUMMER
H 30cm (12in) S 1m (40in)

This vigorous perennial is an ornamental form of clover. Mats of green leaves with contrasting yellow veins are highlighted by fragrant pink flowers. It is useful for filling cracks between paving in partially shaded areas or in a path with stepping stones, but it is too invasive to be planted elsewhere. Bees love it.

Vinca minor Lesser periwinkle
○◐◐○↓↓❖MID-SPRING TO EARLY AUTUMN
H 20cm (8in) S 1m (40in)

Periwinkle's starry, violet-blue flowers light up shady areas. This fast-growing, low-spreading shrub with arching stems is perfect for suppressing weeds on banks and carpeting the ground under deciduous trees and shrubs – anywhere except waterlogged soil. It can be invasive though. *V. major* is a taller cousin of lesser periwinkle. Good varieties: 'La Grave' (large lavender-blue flowers); 'Gertrude Jekyll' (snow-white flowers)

Grasses and bamboos

Ornamental grasses and bamboos are largely sun-worshippers, losing their competitive advantage when grown in shade. However, there are a few true-grass species that can tolerate it, provided they get at least some direct sunlight each day, and even more bamboos that are quite at home in dappled shade.

Some grass-like sedges can cope with the dry, shady conditions found between buildings, while one or two rushes are well adapted to damp, shady areas.

Grasses

Anemanthele lessoniana (syn. Stipa arundinacea)

Pheasant's-tail grass

○ ◐ ◌ ▲ ‖ ❖ YEAR-ROUND

H 1m (40in) S 1.2m (4ft)

A deservedly popular and versatile evergreen grass, if a little invasive. It glows shades of copper, gold and bronze as the summer draws to an end, while dramatic, feathery flowers hang their heads from midsummer until early autumn. Its soft fountain of colour provides lovely textural variety in a mixed or herbaceous border in partial shade. Happy in any soil, but not waterlogged.

Carex buchananii Leatherleaf sedge

○ ◐ ◌ ‖ ❖ YEAR-ROUND

H 60cm (2ft) S 1m (40in)

This tuft-forming sedge looks good surrounded by gravel in a minimalist setting, combined with other shade-tolerant grasses in borders, or on its own in a container. The hair-like coppery leaves provide year-round interest, and brown flower spikes appear from midsummer to autumn.

Carex comans 'Frosted Curls'

○ ◐ ◌ ‖ ❖ YEAR-ROUND

H 60cm (2ft) S 45cm (18in)

The hair-like, silvery-green leaves on this evergreen sedge curl at the tips. Forming tight tussocks, it adds light and form to partially shaded borders. During early and midsummer it produces tiny green flower spikes.

Carex elata 'Aurea' Tufted sedge

○ ◐ ◌ ❖ SPRING TO AUTUMN

H 70cm (28in) S 1m (40in)

The dense clumps of butter-yellow, green-edged leaves of this deciduous perennial sedge look their best in partial shade. Not only is the leaf coloration most impressive in these areas, but the golden glow gives the gloomiest corners a lift. Brown flower spikes appear in early to midsummer. It associates well with shady streams and pools.

Carex flagellifera

○ ◐ ◌ ▲ ‖ ❖ YEAR-ROUND

H 1m (40in) S 90cm (3ft)

A distinctive ornamental sedge with dense mounds of narrow, green to reddish-ginger leaves. Pale-brown flower spikes appear in early to midsummer. It looks good surrounded by gravel in a minimalist setting, or it can be combined with other shade-tolerant grasses in borders. It can also be used in large, permanent tubs, too.

Carex 'Evergold'
○ ◐ ◊ ⬩ ↕↕ ❖ YEAR-ROUND
H and S 25cm (10in)

This versatile ornamental sedge forms low hummocks of striking, dark-green edged, bright creamy-yellow leaves. It produces brown flower spikes from mid-spring to early summer. 'Evergold' makes a great choice for edging borders and containers, and it looks particularly effective planted alongside other ornamental grasses with contrasting foliage.

Carex morrowii 'Variegata'
○ ◐ ◊ ⬩ ↕↕ ❖ YEAR-ROUND
H 60cm (2ft) S 1m (40in)

The striking, white-edged, dark-green leaves of this upright evergreen sedge make it an uplifting understorey plant for gloomy areas. Green or brown flower spikes appear from late spring to early summer. It forms a shimmering, knee-deep ground cover in dappled light under trees, or it can be used as effectiv edging along paths or borders in partial shade.

Carex riparia Greater pond sedge
○ ◐ ◊ ⬩ ❖ YEAR-ROUND
H 1.2m (4ft) S 50cm (20in)

A good evergreen sedge in and around water, with sword-shaped leaves and dark-brown, bristle-tipped flower spikes that last all summer. This is very invasive, so it is unsuitable for small gardens.

Chasmanthium latifolium
Spangle grass
○ ◐ ◊ ⬩ ↕↕ YEAR-ROUND
H 1m (40in) S 60cm (2ft)

A tall, impressive, arching, vase-shaped perennial grass. The lance-shaped leaves take on pinky then straw-yellow shades. Flat, green flower spikes mature to pink and then change to copper tones from midsummer to early autumn. Useful in a partly shaded woodland edge or mixed border.

Deschampsia cespitosa
Tufted hair-grass
○ ◐ ◊ ⬩ ◊ ↕↕ pH↓ −pH→ ❖ YEAR-ROUND
H 2m (6ft) S 1.5m (5ft)

Throughout summer, golden, feathery flower spikes that shimmer in the evening light top tightly packed evergreen tussocks of narrow leaves. The golden froth adds textural contrast to mixed or herbaceous borders in partial shade. For real impact, plant it where it catches the evening sun.

Hakonechloa macra Hakone grass
○ ◐ ◊ ⬩ ↕↕ ❖ YEAR-ROUND
H 35cm (14in) S 40cm (16in)

The tapering, bamboo-like leaves of this slow-spreading perennial grass form emerald-green shaggy mounds, and in autumn take on pink and red shades. What's more, billowing sprays of lime-green flowers appear from early to midsummer. Good varieties: 'Alboaurea' (yellow and green striped leaves); 'Aureola' (shown above)

Helictotrichon sempervirens
Blue oat grass
○◑◐♦◊ ‼ pH→-pH↑ ❖YEAR ROUND
H 1.5m (5ft) S 60cm (2ft)

Golden, summer flower spikes top neat tufts of arching, narrow, blue-grey evergreen leaves in early to midsummer. Although tolerant of light shade, blue oat grass will suffer from rust if it remains wet for too long. Best planted in a minimalist gravel garden or used as a permanent edging plant.

Luzula nivea Snowy woodrush
○–●♦ ‼ ❖YEAR-ROUND
H 60cm (2ft) S 45cm (18in)

The loose clumps of evergreen, downy grey-green foliage of this perennial woodrush provide a shaggy backdrop for the sprays of snow-white, tuft-like flowers in early to midsummer. Slow-spreading, it will eventually form an effective ground-cover plant in shady areas – ideal for defining the edge of a woodland path or covering the ground in deep shade where little else will grow.

Luzula sylvatica Greater woodrush
○–●♦ ‼ ❖YEAR-ROUND
H 80cm (32in) S 45cm (18in)

The evergreen tussocks of lustrous, grass-like, dark-green leaves of this woodrush make excellent weed proof understorey plants for dappled shade. Chestnut-brown flowers appear as a bonus from mid-spring to early summer. This is excellent ground cover for moist, shady areas of the garden – even deep shade. Good varieties: 'Hohe Tatra' (pale-green leaves)

Melica altissima 'Atropurpurea'
Melick
○◑♦ ‼ ❖SPRING TO AUTUMN
H 90cm (3ft) S 50cm (20in)

A deciduous perennial grass that forms loose clumps of pale-green leaves. The unusual, one-sided purple flower spikes produced in early to midsummer fade gradually with age.

Milium effusum 'Aureum'
Bowles' golden grass
●◑♦ ‼ ❖SPRING TO AUTUMN
H 60cm (2ft) S 30cm (12in)

A lovely, tufted, semi-evergreen ornamental perennial grass. Its smooth, strappy, fluorescent golden-yellow leaves shine out in partial shade and the elegant, golden flower spikes bring added interest from late spring to midsummer. Good with purple foliage. Seeds freely.

Sesleria autumnalis Moor grass
○◑♦ ‼ ❖SPRING TO AUTUMN
H 1.2m (4ft) S 60cm (2ft)

Tolerant and easy to grow, this versatile grass forms hummocks of grey-green foliage that supports arching flower spikes on wiry stems from midsummer to mid-autumn. As it is slow-growing and spreading, this is ideal in small gardens. Use to define the edges of woodland paths or soften hard edges in a partially shaded courtyard border.

Bamboos

Fargesia murielae
Umbrella bamboo
○◐◌◑◌ ‖ ❖YEAR-ROUND
H 4m (13ft) S 1.5m (5ft)

This lovely, fountain-shaped bamboo forms miniature clumps of arching canes clothed in small leaves. With its pleasing, softening effect, it looks excellent in containers in a courtyard setting, although it also makes an effective hedge.

Himalayacalamus hookerianus 'Himalaya Blue' Blue bamboo
○◐◌◑◌ ‖ ❖YEAR-ROUND
H 6m (20ft) S 3m (10ft)

A native of cool Himalayan forests, this new, exciting bamboo is well adapted to growing in shade. It is upright-growing with glaucous, blue-green stems that mature to mustard yellow with age. Its limited spread makes it suitable for small gardens, and it's useful for adding vertical interest to shady areas.

Phyllostachys aureosulcata f. *aureocaulis*
Golden-groove bamboo
○◐◌◑◌ ‖ ❖YEAR-ROUND
H 6m (20ft) S 10m (32ft)

Gorgeous orange-yellow canes on this tall and elegant bamboo illuminate lightly shaded borders. Each cane is decorated with occasional green stripes at the base. This is a super specimen, looking especially effective planted where it catches the evening sunlight. Other good varieties: *P. a.* f. *spectabilis* (green-grooved, golden canes)

Phyllostachys nigra Black bamboo
○◐◌◑◌ ‖ ❖YEAR-ROUND
H 5m (16ft) S 3m (10ft)

A fantastic clump-forming bamboo. The elegant, arching green canes, which support dark-green leaves, turn jet-black after two or three years. This looks great in a contemporary, minimalist garden that gets some direct sunlight to ripen and colour the canes fully. It can be grown in large containers, too, provided they are not allowed to dry out.

Pseudosasa japonica
Arrow bamboo
○◐◌◑◌ ‖ ❖YEAR-ROUND
H 6m (20ft) S 8m (27ft)

This is an excellent screening bamboo (and probably the best choice in shady situations), with dark-green, oblong leaves (paler beneath) on vigorous, olive-green canes that turn pale beige with age. It is wind-tolerant too, so it also makes an excellent windbreak.

Sasa palmata Palm bamboo
○–◐◌◑ ‖ ❖YEAR-ROUND
H 2m (6ft) S 6m (20ft)

Exotic-looking and vigorous, this medium-sized bamboo needs to be kept under control. The fresh-green leaves and green canes mean this is just right for creating a lush, jungle feel, or clip it to form knee-deep ground cover in shade – even deep shade.

Ferns

Ferns are perfectly adapted to life in the shade. Provided the soil does not dry out, many can also tolerate direct sunlight, so they are ideal candidates for temporarily shaded borders all around the garden.

Growing conditions

Most ferns will grow in most soils. However, if your soil is very alkaline avoid lime-haters such as the ostrich fern, sensitive fern, royal fern and lady fern. If, on the other hand, your garden soil is acidic you will struggle to grow hart's-tongue ferns or the hard shield and soft shield ferns.

Although very few ferns need constantly moist conditions (and nearly all dislike waterlogged soil), most appreciate an occasional watering during prolonged dry spells. Before planting, incorporate plenty of well-rotted organic matter, such as leaf mould or garden compost, into the soil. If your soil is heavy, mix in a few handfuls of horticultural grit into the planting hole to help aid drainage around the crown.

Mulching is essential with most ferns. Ideally, give them an annual top-dressing of well-rotted organic matter or leaf mould to help keep the root run cool and moist and to prevent competition from weeds.

Uses and positioning

Buckler and shield ferns will thrive in areas that get some direct sun provided they have a cool, moist root run. Others, notably the delicate lady fern and maidenhair fern, will scorch in the midday sun: they are also wind-sensitive, so prefer the extra shelter of surrounding plants.

Ferns can be grown in the border as specimens, collections, or as a knee-deep understorey of ground cover. Many will thrive in dappled light provided their neighbours are not shallow-rooted trees, such as large conifers, beech, ash, elder or willows, which dry out the soil.

A few dwarf ferns, such as *Asplenium scolopendrium* Cristatum Group, are ideal for a shady tub, and moisture-loving types, including the royal fern and ostrich fern, look effective planted alongside natural streams and ponds in a shady woodland garden. Next to manmade water features, where the soil will be drier, choose drought-tolerant ferns such as the male fern.

Ferns are very useful in a shady garden, provided the conditions suit the variety.

Adiantum pedatum
Maidenhair fern
◑💧◊❖SPRING TO AUTUMN
H and S 40cm (16in)

This hardy outdoor fern produces gracefully drooping blue-green ferny fronds on purple stalks from a central clump. It dies down after the first frosts but is good for dry soil in partial shade, such as at the base of a wall, or in a shady corner or general border. Good varieties: 'Japonicum' (coppery-red emerging fronds turn yellow then green)

Adiantum venustum
Himalayan maidenhair fern
●💧◊❖YEAR-ROUND
H 15cm (6in) S 40cm (16in)

This evergreen variety of outdoor maidenhair fern has similar characteristics to *A. pedatum*, though it is smaller in both height and spread.

Asplenium scolopendrium
Hart's-tongue fern

◐◑◐○pH→-pH↑ ❖YEAR-ROUND
H 70cm (28in) S 60cm (2ft)

A lovely clump-forming evergreen fern with glossy, paddle-shaped, bright-green fronds with wavy margins. Hart's tongue likes alkaline soil, so it's useful in borders strewn with rubble next to new-build houses, though it looks attractive in any shady border or patio. Good varieties: Crispum Group; Cristatum Group

Athyrium filix-femina Lady fern

◐◑◐ pH→-pH↓ ❖SPRING TO AUTUMN
H 1.2m (4ft) S 90cm (3ft)

This delightful deciduous clump-forming fern has finely cut, bright-green arching fronds on reddish-brown stems. Good varieties: 'Frizelliae'; 'Minutissimum'; 'Victoriae'

Athyrium niponicum
Japanese painted fern

◐◑◐◐ pH→-pH↓ ❖SPRING TO AUTUMN
H 20cm (8in) S 50cm (20in)

Dapper yet elegant, this deciduous clump-forming fern has deeply cut greyish-green fronds flushed with silver and deep red. It looks effective at woodland edges. Good varieties:
A. n. var. pictum (shown above)

Blechnum penna-marina
Hard fern

○◐◐◐○pH→-pH↓ ❖YEAR-ROUND
H 20cm (8in) S 1m (40in)

In some respects this spreading, low-growing evergreen fern resembles swaying seaweed. Its glossy dark-green leaf fronds are so dense they make an effective weed-suppressing ground cover, especially alongside lined ponds and other water features.

Blechnum spicant Hard fern

○-◐◐ ↓↓pH→-pH↓ ❖SPRING TO AUTUMN
H 50cm (20in) S 60cm (2ft)

The open, spreading, feathery dark-green fronds of this fern form flattened rosettes with age. It looks good in a sheltered woodland edge, shrub or mixed border that does not become waterlogged, and tolerates deep shade.

Dicksonia antarctica
Tasmanian tree fern

◐◑◐❋◐○pH→-pH↓ ❖YEAR-ROUND
H and S 4m (13ft)

A superb tree-like fern with a trunk that's made up of a thick mass of roots topped by arching, ferny fronds. Although ultimately tall, it's very slow-growing – just a couple of centimetres a year – so it's worth buying big if you can. It survives down to -10°C (14°F), but foliage can die back at -2°C (28°F). It looks great in a lightly shaded spot under deciduous trees alongside hardy ferns and other woodland plants.

Dryopteris affinis Golden male fern
◐▲⬦ ‖‖❖YEAR-ROUND
H and S 90cm (3ft)

This native male fern can be found naturalized in woodlands in wetter parts of Britain, although it does not like to be waterlogged. Its handsome shuttlecock form and near-evergreen nature make it an ideal shady garden plant too. Young fronds emerge greenish-gold, giving a springtime fillip, and mature to a darker green. Good varieties: 'Cristata' (arching fronds have crested tips)

Dryopteris erythrosora Buckler fern
◐▲⬦ ‖‖❖SPRING TO AUTUMN
H 60cm (2ft) S 40cm (16in)

The triangular-shaped fronds of this splendid deciduous shuttlecock fern are a lovely copper-red when young; they then turn yellow before slowly maturing to a rich dark green.

Dryopteris filix-mas Male fern
◐▲⬦ ‖❖SPRING TO AUTUMN
H and S 1m (40in)

This large, eye-catching, deciduous shuttlecock fern has feathery green fronds. Although hardy, it needs a spot that is sheltered from strong winds. Good varieties: 'Grandiceps Wills'

Dryopteris wallichiana
Wallich's wood fern
◐▲ ‖‖❖SPRING TO MIDWINTER
H 90cm (3ft) S 75cm (30in)

Although deciduous, this handsome shuttlecock fern remains dark green until midwinter. In spring, it unfurls new greenish-gold fronds that contrast effectively with the scaly black stems and midrib. It makes an excellent addition to a woodland garden, or you can try it in moist shady borders elsewhere.

Gymnocarpium dryopteris
Wood fern
◐▲ ❖SPRING TO AUTUMN
H 20cm (8in) S 1m (40in)

Feathery emerald-green fronds that glow yellowish-green when young characterize this spreading deciduous fern. Try it in moist, shady borders. Good varieties: 'Plumosum' (shown above)

Matteuccia struthiopteris
Ostrich fern
◐▲ pH→-pH↓ ❖YEAR-ROUND
H 1.5m (5ft) S 1m (40in)

Pale-green lacy fronds unfurl in spring then mature to the distinctive shuttlecock shape, and remain a feature in winter. This beautiful deciduous fern looks particularly effective planted next to a natural-looking pond or stream.

Onoclea sensibilis Sensitive fern
◐◖◌ pH→ -pH↓ ❖ SPRING TO AUTUMN
H 60cm (2ft) S 1m (40in)

Reddish-bronze fronds emerge from the upright, arching, bracken-like clumps of this spreading deciduous fern before maturing to green.

Osmunda regalis Royal fern
◐◖ pH→ -pH↓ ❖ SPRING TO AUTUMN
H 2m (6ft) S 4m (13ft)

Large and handsome, this deciduous, moisture-loving fern produces bright-green lacy-edged fronds that turn bronze in autumn. It associates well with natural-looking water features, such as a pond or stream.

Polypodium vulgare Wall fern
◐●◖◌ pH→ -pH↑ ❖ YEAR-ROUND
H 30cm (12in) S 80cm (32in)

This is a robust, compact evergreen fern with deeply cut, triangular-shaped dark-green feathery fronds. It does well in any shady situation, including containers, and copes well with dry soil. Sometimes colonizes cracks in a north-facing wall, provided it is sheltered from cold winds. Good varieties: 'Bifidocristatum'; 'Cornubiense Grandiceps'

Polystichum aculeatum Hard shield fern
◐●◖◌ ↓↓ pH→ -pH↑ ❖ YEAR-ROUND
H 60cm (2ft) S 90cm (3ft)

With its long, deep-green fronds, this reliable evergreen fern forms a distinctive shuttlecock-like shape. It looks good in winter, too, when the finely divided foliage is decorated by a hoar frost. As it's particularly hardy, this is useful for all-year interest against north-facing walls and fences, even where there is deep shade.

Polystichum setiferum Soft shield fern
◐●◖ pH→ -pH↑ 🍃 ❖ YEAR-ROUND
H 1.2m (4ft) S 90cm (3ft)

This large, evergreen, shuttlecock-shaped fern with soft, dark-green fronds likes partial shade such as a sheltered woodland edge, shrub or a mixed border, but it will also grow in deep shade in humus-rich soil. Good varieties: Divisilobum Group; 'Divisilobum Iveryanum'; Plumosodivisilobum Group (shown above)

Thelypteris palustris Marsh fern
◐◖ pH→ -pH↑ ❖ SPRING TO AUTUMN
H 60cm (2ft) S 1m (40in)

Shaggy and spreading in habit, this deciduous fern produces paddle-shaped, pale-green fronds. It's a useful addition to a woodland garden or in moist, shady borders elsewhere.

Bedding plants

Old-fashioned bedding schemes aren't to everyone's taste, but their sheer flower-power can be an important ingredient in the shady garden. You don't have to use them the traditional way, of course, and they can be selected to complement an existing scheme.

Not all bedding plants will perform in shade. Indeed, most summer bedding needs good light and moist soil to grow and flower well. However, there are several popular types that can cope with being shaded for at least part of the day or will grow happily in dappled light, provided the soil does not dry out.

In areas of deep shade your choice is really limited to varieties of impatiens and *Begonia semperflorens,* which do surprisingly well. For partially shaded dry soil, try pelargonium (bedding geraniums) and calendulas.

All the plants listed here can be grown in containers, which can be circulated around the garden, spending part of their time in the shade with 'holidays' in the sun.

Spring bedding

The following spring bedding, plus pansies and Brompton stocks (*see page 114*), will grow in partial shade. Sow in late spring to early summer, then plant out in early autumn for flowers between early spring and early summer.

■ Forget-me-nots (*Myosotis*) actually prefer moist partial shade and are prolific self-seeders. You can buy individual flower colours (blue, white or pink) to suit particular colour schemes and they are ideal for underplanting beneath summer-flowering deciduous shrubs to extend the season of interest.

■ Double daisies (*Bellis*) will also perform well in partial shade and are ideal for edging borders and adding colour to containers. They can be bought as mixtures or individual colours, depending on the variety.

Ageratum Floss flower
○ ◐ ❀ ◌ ◍ ⬩⬩ ❖EARLY SUMMER TO EARLY AUTUMN
H and S 20cm (8in)

Low-growing, compact mounds of downy leaves carry long-lasting fluffy heads of flowers. Good in dappled shade where soil doesn't dry out (but avoid the 'drip zone' at the edges of shrubs, since the flowers tend to rot if they remain wet for long periods). Good varieties: 'Blue Mink' (azure-blue flowers: shown above)

Antirrhinum Snapdragon
○ ◐ ❀ ◌ ◍ ⬩⬩ ❖EARLY SUMMER TO EARLY AUTUMN
H and S 30cm (12in)

Snapdragon produces superb spikes of flowers, variable in size, shape and colour. Look for compact, rust-resistant varieties and dead-head routinely, cutting back flowered spikes to a lower sideshoot, which will flower later.

Begonia semperflorens Begonia
○–● ❀ ◌ ◍ ⬩⬩ ❖SUMMER TO AUTUMN
H and S 30cm (12in)

Begonia has superb coppery-bronze foliage and beautiful flowers in a range of colours from white to deep red. Dead-head, if you have the patience, to keep displays looking good and to prevent fading blooms rotting on the plant in shade. Good in all types of situations, including containers, with soil that doesn't dry out. Good varieties: 'Cocktail' (shown above); 'Party Fun'

Calendula Pot marigold
○ ◐ ❀ ◌ ◍ ⬩⬩ ❖EARLY SUMMER TO MID-AUTUMN
H 30cm (12in) S 45cm (18in)

Sunny, bright-yellow, gold and orange double flowers shine out above aromatic, fresh-green foliage. Marigolds are easy to grow, but produce fewer flowers in damp conditions and can be susceptible to mildew. Useful in partially shaded spots at the base of walls or in dry soil in dappled light. Good varieties: Fiesta Gitana Group (shown above); 'Kablouna' (gold, orange, lemon and apricot flowers)

Impatiens Busy Lizzie

○–● ❋◆💧 ↕↕ ❖EARLY SUMMER TO EARLY AUTUMN
H and **S** 30cm (12in)

An amazingly adaptable bedding plant that will thrive in all light conditions, provided the soil doesn't dry out. Dazzling, long-lasting blooms in a variety of colours from white to deep red are produced over pale-green, toothed leaves on fleshy stems. Ideal shady-container plants. Good varieties: 'Double Carousel' (double flowers); 'Super Elfin Picotee Swirl'; Tempo series (apricot to deep red: shown above)

Matthiola Stock

○◐ ❋💧 ↕↕ pH➤–pH↑ ❖ SUMMER
H 45cm (18in) **S** 30cm (12in)

Deliciously spice-scented spikes of summer flowers, often with pale, even silvery, foliage. May need staking in shady conditions. Stocks are superb alongside partially shaded paths and doorways or next to shady seating areas. Useful gap-fillers too. Good varieties: 'Brompton Stock' (pink, purple and white flowers: shown above); 'Dwarf Ten Week Stock' (white, cream, yellow, pink and purple flowers)

Pelargonium Bedding geranium

○◐ ❋💧◊ ↕↕ ❖EARLY SUMMER TO MID-AUTUMN
H and **S** 30cm (12in)

This provides reliable flower-power for lightly shaded areas with dry soil. Different varieties come in a range of eye-catching colours – snow-white to blood-red – with aromatic, fleshy, bright-green foliage. Improve displays by removing yellowing leaves and regular dead-heading. It is also a superb container plant. Good varieties: Multibloom series (shown above); Sensation series

Lobelia Lobelia

○◐ ❋💧◊ ↕↕ ❖LATE SUMMER TO MID-AUTUMN
H 10cm (4in) **S** 15cm (6in)

Neat, spreading mounds of airy, bronze-flushed, dark-green leaves are smothered in tiny colourful flowers with a contrasting white eye. Lightly trim plants if they become leggy in shade. A superb edging plant in partially shaded areas. Good varieties: 'Mrs Clibran' (deep-blue flowers); 'Red Cascade' (purple-red flowers: shown above); 'White Cascade' (trailing, white flowers)

Nicotiana sylvestris
Tobacco plant

○◐ ❋💧 ↕↕ ❖MIDSUMMER TO EARLY AUTUMN
H 1.5m (5ft) **S** 60cm (2ft)

This old-fashioned tobacco plant bears dramatic heads of deliciously fragrant, snow-white trumpets on towering stems. The aroma is released at dusk, so plant around the patio and other seating areas to perfume the air on summer evenings. Good varieties: Domino series (modern, compact, unscented varieties in a range of pastel colours – ideal for containers and edging borders)

Viola Pansy

○◐💧◊ ↕↕ ❖YEAR-ROUND
H 15cm (6in) **S** 30cm (12in)

Pansies are popular for their brightly coloured flowers above fresh-green foliage. By combining the right varieties you can have pansies in bloom almost all year. Ideal edging for borders and pots, but don't let the compost dry out. Good varieties: 'Imperial Frosty Rose' (rose-purple flowers, early spring to midsummer); 'Universal Mixed' (purple, yellow, red and white flowers, early winter to early spring)

Trees

Even in a shady garden there are plenty of reasons why you might want to plant a tree: as part of an overall design – perhaps to give height and structure; to make a striking focal point; to replace a tree that has died; or because you want that extra bit of shade in years to come just where there isn't any to sit under now. Most of the trees listed here will grow in full sun or partial shade, so they can be used for any of these purposes.

Choosing trees

Trees are long-term investments that will have a dramatic impact on the garden design, therefore it is essential to choose a variety that not only looks good for much of the year, but is well behaved so doesn't cause problems with its roots, shoots or leaves. For example, it is easy to be seduced by the stunning sugar-pink blossom offered by many flowering cherries in spring, but the display will only last a week or two and many varieties have invasive, suckering roots.

A better option would be a flowering crab apple, such as *Malus* 'John Downie', which offers snow-white blossom during late spring, followed by red and orange fruits that last into autumn. It's fast-growing but stops when it reaches about 10m (32ft) in height and 6m (20ft) in spread.

When choosing a tree, shop around for the best value as prices can vary between suppliers. If you want a large tree for instant impact,

go to a specialist grower who can help you transport and plant it. Make sure the tree is healthy with no signs of pest or disease and is not pot-bound or neglected – avoid trees with roots curling around the bottom of the rootball and weeds growing in the compost.

Acer capillipes Snake-bark maple
○ ◐ ◐ 💧 ‡‡ ❖ YEAR- ROUND
H and S 10m (32ft)

This lovely spreading tree has greenish-brown bark, intricately streaked with white, that looks great all year. In spring, new shoots are coral-red, with bright-green three-pointed leaves, which look attractive throughout the summer before turning dramatic, fiery shades of red in autumn. Superb garden value and a fine specimen tree for a small to medium garden.

Acer griseum Paper-bark maple
○ ◐ ◐ 💧 ‡‡ ❖ YEAR-ROUND
H and S 10m (32ft)

Prized for its polished, mahogany-red peeling bark that looks stunning in winter, this slow-growing, spreading tree also looks good at other times. In autumn, its deeply lobed, dark-green leaves turn fiery shades of orange, red and scarlet. This is a perfect specimen tree for a small to medium garden.

Acer negundo 'Flamingo'
Box elder
○ ◐ ◐ 💧 ❖ SPRING TO AUTUMN
H 15m (48ft) S 10m (32ft)

Not everybody's cup of tea, but an eye-catching specimen tree nonetheless. This ash-leaved maple has light-green leaves that emerge edged in pink, maturing to white in summer. Clusters of greenish-yellow flowers in mid- to late spring are a bonus. Fast-growing, and forming a rounded to spreading outline, this makes a startling element in a medium garden.

Trees for acid soil

Amelanchier lamarckii
(June berry)

Sorbus aucuparia 'Aspleniifolia'
(mountain ash)

Stewartia pseudocamellia

Amelanchier lamarckii June berry

○ ◐ ◑ pH↓ 🍃 ❖ SPRING, AUTUMN
H 10m (32ft) S 12m (39ft)

An excellent-value garden tree with attractive emerging bronze foliage that matures to dark green, as well as spring flowers and superb autumn colour in shades of orange and red. But it's the star-shaped, airy white flowers that appear in early to mid-spring that really catch the eye. Great for providing shade in a sunny garden or for adding height to an acid border in a shady one.

Betula pendula 'Youngii'
Young's weeping birch

○ ◐ ◑ ↓↓ ❖ YEAR-ROUND
H 8m (26ft) S 6m (20ft)

Glinting, diamond-shaped, bright-green leaves cast lovely dancing shadows under this weeping birch before turning butter yellow in autumn. The peeling snow-white bark looks good all year, while attractive yellowish-brown catkins are a feature during early spring. Fast-growing but relatively short-lived, this dwarf tree is an acquired taste!

Betula utilis var. *jacquemontii*
West Himalayan birch

○ ◐ ◑ ↓↓ ❖ SPRING, AUTUMN
H 18m (59ft) S 10m (32ft)

This lovely, elegant tree is known for its dazzling white bark. Its dark-green leaves on flexible stalks dance in the breeze, creating shimmering shadows below. Yellowish-brown catkins are a feature in spring and the leaves turn butter yellow in autumn. 'Jermyns' is a particularly good form.

Cornus controversa Dogwood

○ ◐ ◑ ↓↓ ❖ SPRING, AUTUMN
H and S 15m (48ft)

Eye-catching tiered branches make this deciduous dogwood a striking specimen tree. Cow-parsley-like heads of white, early-summer flowers stand out against the glossy leaves, followed by blue-black fruit. By autumn, the tree is a beacon of reds and purples. Good varieties: 'Variegata' (cream-edged leaves: shown above)

Cornus 'Eddie's White Wonder'
Dogwood

○ ◐ ◑ ↓↓ pH→ -pH↓ ❖ SPRING, AUTUMN
H 6m (20ft) S 5m (16ft)

A head-turning spectacle in late spring when covered in flower-like white bracts surrounding inconspicuous, purplish-green flowers. This conical tree (performing best in full sun) is attractive at other times too, with the leaves turning orange, red and purple in autumn. Excellent for a small garden.

Crataegus laevigata 'Paul's Scarlet' Hawthorn

○ ◐ ◑ ○ ↓↓ ❖ SPRING, AUTUMN
H and S 8m (26ft)

A profusion of double, deep-pink blossom – in tight clusters on branches of deeply lobed, glossy, dark-green leaves – appears in mid- to late spring. Spherical red fruit follows. This rounded, thorny, deciduous tree is as tough as old boots, and can cope with exposed sites, city pollution and even salt-laden air.

Eucalyptus pauciflora subsp. *niphophila* Snow gum
○◐💧‖❖YEAR-ROUND
H and S 6m (20ft)

This is a small eucalyptus tree with attractive peeling bark and leathery, lance-shaped grey-blue foliage, which casts a delightful shadow in a hot and sunny garden. The stems have a waxy white bloom. A superb specimen in a small south-facing garden, it is particularly effective when grown as a multi-stemmed tree.

Gleditsia triacanthos 'Sunburst'
Honey locust
○💧◊‖❖SPRING TO AUTUMN
H 12m (39ft) S 10m (32ft)

An open, airy, broadly conical deciduous tree that casts wonderful shadows. This thornless, fast-growing variety has ferny foliage that matures to rich green and turns butter yellow in autumn. Great in a small south-facing garden. Other good varieties: 'Rubylace' (purple foliage)

Malus hupehensis
Chinese crab apple
○◐💧◊‖SPRING TO AUTUMN
H and S 12m (39ft)

This magnificent spreading crab apple, with dark-green leaves on stiff branches that cast great shade, comes from China. In mid- to late spring masses of fragrant white blossom opens from pink buds, followed by cherry-sized red fruits. Just the job for a small or medium garden.

Malus 'John Downie'
Crab apple
○◐💧◊‖❖SPRING TO AUTUMN
H 10m (32ft) S 6m (20ft)

A particularly fine ornamental crab apple, smothered in pale-pink buds that open to reveal snow-white blossom during late spring. This fast-growing tree looks good in autumn, too, when laden with edible red and orange fruits. It performs best in full sun, but it is one of the best specimen trees for a small garden.

Malus × *robusta* 'Red Sentinel'
Crab apple
○◐💧◊‖❖LATE SPRING, WINTER
H and S 6m (20ft)

A star of the winter garden when laden with glossy red, cherry-sized apples, this excellent crab also looks the part during late spring when tricked out with pretty, pink-flushed white blossom. Pollution tolerant.

Prunus 'Amanogawa'
Japanese flowering cherry
○◐💧◊‖❖SPRING TO AUTUMN
H 8m (26ft) S 4m (13ft)

Multi-stemmed upright or columnar tree that's covered in clusters of fragrant, semi-double shell-pink blossoms during mid-spring. One of the best Japanese cherries as its flowers last longer than most, it looks good in summer, and offers autumn tints too. This is a good choice for late-spring impact in a small garden, but it performs best in full sun.

Prunus sargentii Sargent cherry
◯◐◖◇ ‼❖ SPRING TO AUTUMN
H 20m (66ft) **S** 15m (48ft)

This spreading, deciduous, ornamental cherry casts great shade when clothed in deep-red foliage that turns fiery red in autumn. A bonus of shell-pink, mid- to late-spring blossom is followed by a reliable crop of glossy red fruits. It is a a lovely tree for a medium garden.

Prunus × *subhirtella* 'Autumnalis' Autumn cherry
◯◖◇ ‼❖ WINTER TO MID-SPRING
H and **S** 8m (26ft)

A brilliant winter-flowering cherry that produces masses of pinkish-white flowers, which continue on and off during mild spells to mid-spring. This forms an attractive, domed tree at other times with dark-green leaves casting good shade. Other good varieties: 'Pendula Plena Rosea' (rose-pink flowers, weeping habit)

Robinia pseudoacacia 'Frisia'
False acacia
◯◖◇ ‼❖ SPRING TO AUTUMN
H 15m (48ft) **S** 8m (26ft)

Glowing butter-yellow foliage casts lovely shade under this airy columnar tree. The leaves develop orangey tones in autumn. During late spring and early summer clusters of fragrant white flowers are an added treat. Ideal in a small, sunny, sheltered garden.

Sorbus aria 'Lutescens'
Whitebeam
◯◐◖◇ ‼❖ SPRING TO AUTUMN
H 10m (32ft) **S** 8m (26ft)

This is an uplifting tree for partial shade where the silvery young leaves on purple shoots shine out. Even in summer the grey-green foliage looks great, and late-spring white flowers are another plus, followed by orange-red berries in autumn. Perfect for a small garden.

Sorbus aucuparia 'Aspleniifolia'
Mountain ash
◯◐◖◇ ‼ pH▶-pH↓ ❖ SPRING, AUTUMN
H 15m (48ft) **S** 7m (23ft)

The attractive ferny foliage of this broad, pyramid-forming tree turns dark red and yellow in autumn. During mid- to late spring the branches are smothered in delicate sprays of snow-white flowers, followed in autumn by generous bunches of bright-red berries, which are devoured by birds. Good for a wildlife garden or as part of a mini-woodland. Pollution tolerant.

Stewartia pseudocamellia
◐◖ pH▶-pH↓ 🍂 ❖ SPRING TO AUTUMN
H 20m (64ft) **S** 8m (26ft)

Decorative, peeling bark is one of the charms of this lovely pyramid-shaped deciduous tree. Its finely toothed, dark-green foliage turns shades of yellow, orange and red in autumn. As a bonus, frilly-edged white flowers appear from mid- to late summer. This is a very slow-growing tree.

A gardening calendar

In a shady garden, pruning to promote the best foliage and flowering displays, recycling fallen leaves, controlling moss and algae, and staying vigilant for pests such as slugs and snails are particularly important. However, as with any other type of garden, it's also good to know when is the best time to plant new specimens, take cuttings and sow seed, stake perennials and protect vulnerable plants, as well as all the other routine but essential tasks in the gardening year. No matter how long you've been gardening, it's useful to have a memory jogger for when to do what.

Spring and summer

With spring comes an explosion of new growth – and plenty of work to do. The fun bit is of course sowing and planting, but, as the season progresses into summer, feeding and watering become the main priorities – and of course you'll need to keep on top of those weeds and that moss.

Early spring

At this time of year all actively growing border plants will benefit from a top-dressing of organic fertilizer such as blood, fish and bone, especially on poor soils.

Apply a 5–7cm (2–3in) layer of composted bark chippings or proprietary mulch over bare soil between plants to help suppress weeds and conserve soil moisture.

New plants Inspect perennials and lift and divide overcrowded or poorly performing clumps. Fleshy-rooted shade-lovers, such as hostas, can be left until the new growth appears above ground.

Lawns Make the first lawn cut in milder areas (wait a month elsewhere). On a mild day trim shady lawns when the grass reaches about 8cm (3in), setting the mower to remove about 2–3cm (¾–1in). Thereafter, cut when it reaches 4cm (1½in), removing just 1cm (½in) with each cut.

Rake moss out of lawns in shade and spike the area to improve surface drainage.

Pruning Prune shrubs that flower on new growth by cutting back all last year's growth to about two buds. Cut shrubs grown for their decorative stems, such as cornus, salix and rubus, right back to near ground level. Now is also a good time to prune overgrown shade-tolerant shrubs, such as *Prunus laurocerasus* and *P. lusitanica*.

Mid-spring

With all the fresh growth at this time of year, the slugs and snails will be having a field day. Protect susceptible

You'll need to be vigilant in spring to stop snails and slugs ruining the new leaves of their favourite plants.

plants in shady borders by trapping or hand-picking these pests.

Keep all new plants well watered. Established plants growing in dry soil at the foot of walls will also need water.

Tall-growing border perennials benefit from being staked now, before the growth is too advanced.

New plants Plants, cuttings and seedlings raised under cover will need acclimatizing by hardening off over the next few weeks. Gradually increase ventilation and lower the temperature, first during the day and then at night-time, too.

Remove the fading flowers from spring-flowering bulbs, but leave the foliage to die down naturally – trimming or tying it up will reduce the ability of the bulbs to photosynthesize and will seriously impair future flowering performance.

New, hardy deciduous shrubs and trees, as well as herbaceous plants and climbers, can be planted now. Plant conifers too.

This is the time to sow hardy annuals and half-hardy annuals. In mild areas, hardy annuals can be sown direct into well-prepared soil outside; wait a month elsewhere.

Pruning Carefully dead-head early rhododendrons and azaleas. Remove the dead flowers and end-leaf rosettes from mahonia to encourage bushiness and more flowering.

Containers Plant containers with early-summer bedding, or make up a pot with herbs that can tolerate a bit of shade. Prick out earlier sowings as necessary.

Late spring
Clear moss and algae from shady paths, steps and patios, using a pressure washer or a stiff broom and soapy water.

Staking heavy-headed or floppy plants in spring ensures a well-supported display come summer.

Pruning Clip fast-growing hedges such as Leyland cypress and privet every few weeks from now until late summer to keep neat and tidy. Prune informal hedges after flowering.

After flowering, cut back spring-flowering clematis (pruning group 1).

Containers Fresh compost has sufficient nutrients to feed new plants for about six weeks. After that, apply a liquid feed regularly, or add a slow-release fertilizer to the compost, which will last the whole season. Don't neglect the watering.

Lawns Make the first cut of shady lawns planted with naturalized bulbs, setting the blade as high as possible. Gradually reduce the blade height every couple of weeks.

Plant up hanging baskets in mid-spring along with other containers, but keep an eye out for late frosts.

It is possible to sow grass seed now, although autumn is the better time as there is less competion from weeds. Protect from birds.

Early summer
This is the time of year when many diseases take hold or start to become apparent. Roses in particular will be more stressed in shady gardens and more likely to succumb to disease. Grow disease-resistant varieties.

New plants It is now safe to plant out tender plants.

Many shrubs can be propagated now from new sideshoots (softwood cuttings), while new climbers can be raised from stem cuttings.

Divide primulas and polyanthus after flowering.

Pruning Prune overcrowded or poorly performing early-flowering shrubs to rejuvenate them.

Early-summer bedding will flower for longer if the fading blooms are removed regularly.

Dead-head repeat-flowering climbing roses; remove any suckers.

Midsummer

This is the ideal time to take note of any trees and shrubs that are causing shade problems (this is less obvious in the winter months). Wait until the dormant season before taking action.

New plants Pick ripening seedheads and dry them upside down in paper bags in a cool, dry place. Label the bags clearly.

Shade-tolerant autumn-flowering bulbs such as hardy cyclamen, colchicums and autumn crocus can be planted now.

Many shade-loving ground-cover plants, such as ajuga (bugle), ivy and periwinkle, can be propagated

easily now. This is a cost-effective way of raising a lot of plants.

Some shade-loving shrubs (such as azaleas) and shade-tolerant climbers (such as clematis) can be propagated from layers.

Shade-loving biennials – forget-me-nots, foxgloves and polyanthus are good choices – can be sown in pots or a part of the garden where they won't be disturbed. Move the young plants to their flowering position in autumn or early spring.

Late summer

New plants Summer cuttings using semi-ripe shoots can be taken from many shrubs and climbers at this time. Also take cuttings from tender perennials as insurance against winter losses.

Here, lychnis seeds are being harvested. A number of perennials are suitable for seed collection, including the shade lovers alchemilla, aquilegia, foxgloves, euphorbia, hellebores, heuchera, rodgersia and tellima. It's a great way to save money, and many clubs and societies run exchange schemes.

Towards the end of summer trim evergreen hedges back into shape, or try your hand at a bit of topiary with good-natured box.

Pruning and training Varieties of rambler rose that flower in one flush, such as 'Albertine', can be pruned now that flowering is over. Cut back one old stem for every new vigorous shoot produced this year.

Trim all formal beech, box, holly, hornbeam, laurel, yew, Leyland cypress and Lawson's cypress hedges now. Cut back any informal hedges not already pruned.

Prune back the new growth of wisteria to five leaves. Tie in escallonia and other wall shrubs.

Tie new, whippy shoots produced by many climbers into their supports to prevent them being damaged in windy weather.

Don't forget

Throughout the summer, you need to keep an eye on moisture levels. Priority plants are those in containers, new specimens and anything growing in dry areas, such as next to walls. Water honeysuckle to help prevent mildew.

Autumn and winter

These seasons are for catching up on maintenance tasks in the garden and preparing for the following year so you get off to a good, early start in springtime, when it's all systems go again.

Early to mid-autumn

The main priority now is to prepare for the first frosts of autumn. Protect tender plants with garden fleece. Close-weave netting can help to protect not-so-hardy climbers and shrubs. Move potted tender plants undercover and dig up any tender bulbs and move them to a safe place.

New plants Set out pansies, primulas and polyanthus now so that they can become well established before the onset of winter. Plant new trees, shrubs and climbers.

Plant shade-tolerant spring-flowering bulbs such as crocus, snowdrops and species daffodils.

Propagate fast-growing deciduous shrubs by taking hardwood cuttings.

If you are intending to grow annuals, biennials and perennials from seed next year, order catalogues and make your selections by midwinter.

Lawns Re-seed bare patches and repair broken edges. Rake out thatch from vigorously growing areas of grass and aerate compacted lawns with a fork.

Clear fallen leaves from shady lawns regularly – use your mower to collect and chop up the leaves ready for composting in black sacks – or, in a large garden, construct a leaf-mould bin.

Late autumn to early winter

Dig any areas of the garden that have been cleared in preparation for planting. Heavy soils benefit from digging now as the large clods can be broken down by frosts.

Pruning Cut back the side shoots on wisteria, shortening them to two or three buds – about finger length.

Containers The need for watering plants in permanent containers will be reduced now, but carry on if the weather is dry.

Remove dead flowerheads and old foliage. Tidy up and divide large, fibrous-rooted perennials.

Towards the end of the season, protect susceptible container plants with bubble-wrap.

Mid- to late winter

At this time of year, the watchword is preparation. Dig over areas you are planning to plant or sow, including areas for a new lawn. Then cover the ground with clear polythene to warm the soil and encourage any weed seeds to germinate so that they can be removed.

Prepare for early sowings by checking propagation equipment is in good order. Put up insulation and check that the greenhouse heater is functioning.

Shady gardens usually mean lots of leaves: turn them into free compost.

New plants When the weather is fine and the soil workable, plant deciduous trees and shrubs. Check too that recently planted specimens haven't been lifted by frost and re-firm if necessary. Inspect tree ties and stakes to make sure they are secure but not constricting.

Pruning Prune late-summer flowering clematis (pruning group 3) now. Early-summer flowering varieties can be lightly pruned too.

Prune bush roses just before new shoots break in late winter or early spring, depending on the weather and where you live. After pruning, if the weather is mild, mulch with well-rotted manure or compost.

Index

Page numbers in *italics* refer to plants illustrated and described in the 'Plants for shade' chapter.

Acknowledgements

BBC Books and OutHouse would like to thank the following for their
assistance in preparing this book: Andrew McIndoe for his advice and
guidance; Helena Caldon and Joanne Forrest Smith for picture
research; Julia Brittain for proofreading; Marie Lorimer for the index.

Picture credits

Key   t = top, b = bottom, l = left, r = right, c = centre

All photographs by Jonathan Buckley except the following:

Alamy Jim Allan 113tc; CuboImages/Paroli Galperti 87bc

DK Images 82tr; Deni Bown 113tr, 110bc; Andrew Henley 114tl;
Andrew Lawson 114tr; Roger Smith 110tr

GAP Photos 106bl; Pernilla Bergdahl 80bl, 92tr, 117br; Adrian Bloom
101br, 107tc; Richard Bloom 76tl; 111tl; Mark Bolton 15b, 33, 77tl & bc,
84bc; Elke Borkowski 57t, 66T, 89br; Jonathan Buckley 76; Leigh Clapp
58br; Paul Debois 93bl; Carole Drake 19t, 110bl; Tim Gainey 118bc, 120t;
John Glover 75tl, 76bl, 77tr, 100bc, 101bl, 107br, 114tc, 118br;
FhF Greenmedia 86bl, 101tr; Jerry Harpur 18B, 20, 77bl, 114bc; Marcus
Harpur 107bc; Derek Harris 102bc; Neil Holmes 82bl, 85bc, 87tc, bl & br,
88tl; Lynn Keddie 35; Geoff Kidd 97tc, 103tr & bl, 108br, 109br; Andrew
Lawson 77tc; Zara Napier 34, 74bc, 122t; Clive Nichols 88tr, 108tl, 108tr,
116tr; Howard Rice 32, 96tr; JS Sira 76tc, 85tc, 95tr; 111tr, 113bc; Nicola
Stocken Tomkins 102tr; Maddie Thornhill 112bc; Jo Whitworth 19b;
Rob Whitworth 85tl, 107bl; Visions 86tl, 112br, 116bl, 117br, 118tr

The Garden Collection Torie Chugg 113br; Liz Eddison 114br;
Andrew Lawson 114bc;

Garden World Images FloraMedia 87tr

Getty Images David Sanger 108bl

John Glover 103tl, 117bl

Harpur Garden Library 61tr, 84bc, 106tr

Andrew McIndoe 84tl, 85tr, 84bl

Clive Nichols 93tl

Photolibrary Group Frederic Didillon 12t; Ron Evans 11; AGE
Fotostock 10t; Francois De Heel 9t; Jean-Claude Hurni 13; Dufour
Brigette Dit Noun 28, 49

Science Photo Library Rosemary Greenwood 106tc; MF Merlet
93bl; Adrian Thomas 114bl

Thanks are also due to the following designers and owners whose
gardens appear in the book:

Fiona Bruce, RHS Chelsea Flower Show 2005 29b. David Chase 99.
Marie Clarke 8. Mhairi Clutson 15t. Ellen Mary Fenton & Neil Malachy
Black, RHS Chelsea Flower Show 2005 27b. Fergus Garrett 9b. Anthony
Goff 10b. Jean Goldberry 27t. Bunny Guinness 43t. Jim Honey & James
Dyson, RHS Chelsea Flower Show 2003 48. Paul Kelly 10t. Christopher
Lloyd, Great Dixter, East Sussex 73, 94. John Massey, Ashwood
Nurseries, Staffordshire 12b, 14b, 22b, 26b, 38. Christopher Masson 20.
Natural & Oriental Water Gardens 108tl. Bob Parker, Broad Lane,
Wolverhampton, Staffordshire 31b. Judy Pearce, Lady Farm, Somerset
47b. Bob Purnell 84bc. Sarah Raven, Perch Hill, East Sussex 30, 69.
David and Mavis Seeney 16b. Carol & Malcolm Skinner, Eastgrove
Cottage Garden Nursery, Worcestershire 17bl, 18t, 29t. Sue & Wol
Staines, Glen Chantry, Essex 37, 68, 119, 120b. Peter Thurman 19b.
Sue Ward, Ladywood, Hampshire 31t, 121. Wayford Manor, Somerset
109bl. Wynniatt-Husey Clarke 108tr. Helen Yemm: Eldenhurst, East
Sussex 16t; Ketley's, East Sussex 26t, 52.

While every effort has been made to trace and acknowledge all
copyright holders, the publisher would like to apologize should
there be any errors or omissions.